LESSONS IN
Humility
40 YEARS OF TEACHING

BARRY DICKINS

Published in 2013 by Connor Court Publishing Pty Ltd

Copyright © Barry Dickins 2013

ALL RIGHTS RESERVED. This book contains material protected under International and Federal Copyright Laws and Treaties. Any unauthorised reprint or use of this material is prohibited. No part of this book may be reproduced or transmitted in any form or by any means, electronic or mechanical, including photocopying, recording, or by any information storage and retrieval system without express written permission from the publisher.

Connor Court Publishing Pty Ltd.
PO Box 1
Ballan VIC 3342
sales@connorcourt.com
www.connorcourt.com

ISBN: 9781922168009 (pbk.)

Cover design by Ian James, front cover sketch by Barry Dickins. Sketches in book also by Barry Dickins.

Printed in Australia

CONTENTS

Introduction

I The Beginning: Forty Years Ago   1
   The School Camp   23
   The Mountain Country   35

II The More-or-Less Present   39
   Blueberry Primary   43
   Posh College   49
   The Paucity of Dreams   67
   Aniseed North South High   74
   A Bit of a Fright in the Street   83
   Mull   85
   Saint Ursula's   94

III Boil Street Special School Revisited   107
   Why Exactly it is that Weekends are Worse for Teachers?   116
   The Epitome of Learning   125
   The Defeat Gene   135
   School Camp II   143
   The Carpet Shampoo Freak   149
   A Particularly Difficult Girl   175
   Tram Jack   179

Tuning in to Only Nature was my Teacher's Breakthrough	191
The Pure Horror of Collaboration	204
An Eternal Meeting	225
The Review	235
The House of Welcome	241
The Learning Lies in Eyes	245

Introduction

Above all this book is true. It is never a cartoon of teaching or a caricature of education. The writing is faithful to the theme of the ongoing warfare between dedicated teachers and illiterate children. They don't wish to learn and the teachers intend them to.

I have taught for my living since graduation around forty years ago. At its best teaching guarantees love because you can't describe the feeling any other way. By remaining open-minded and digging the wax out of your ears, you can get through to kids and help them obtain work after they leave school.

At its worst you feel used-up, degraded, defeated and all screwed-up because of the abuse of you, the contempt for you, the nausea you feel merely entering the minefield of a grubby and claustrophobic classroom. I have done my teachers-rounds at a community school where two girls in my year committed suicide due to the hopelessness and sheer frustration they felt there.

When I completed my Dip. Ed. all those decades ago nobody actually taught you how to teach, how to hold barbarians' limited attention. You simply suffered all the time, if you were nice, born friendly as I was myself, out of a friendly mother and honest hardworking father who always lectured me before breakfast by saying to me still in bed at 5am, 'You have to get a few runs on the board in this life. No one else can do it for you.'

My efforts to teach thugs and harpies is contained

within these spectral pages. I have always experienced difficulty separating life from theatre and have often found some aspects of daily existence pretty hard to take in, such as the vile way kids address those who simply want them educated otherwise there is a very real danger they shall end up under a bridge, or even six feet under.

Being a maverick without meaning to be I have clashed with brutal and brutalised school children as well as sometimes intellectually connecting with them. Sometimes the staff at schools where I've taught are more remote or even stupider than the kids who can't add up two and two.

I have taught very poor under-funded primary schools my interpretation of English and spontaneous prose and poem-composition in the morning from 8.40 am until noon and then motored across town from West Preston Primary where I experienced loss of hearing after one hour of the grade twos and ended up teaching the second half of the day at Posh College, so I have known very acutely the class divide in schools, and the arrogance of the innumerate rich.

I have always kept a diary with me no matter where I have taught and this memoir is really the edited low lights of it, with a few snatches of beauty thrown in. I have had my nose broken for me at an inner city community college when two physical education instructors allowed Year Ten kids to play indoor soccer right where I was teaching silk screen printing. I caught the tram to the hospital and had it re-set and the nurses were very nice to me and handed me an aspririn.

I went back to work next day with a plaster cast over my broken face and not one single teacher asked me how I was going. That's the problem with society today. We never ask each other how we're going. Do we?

The angels and grotesques contained in these paragraphs exist not in satire but reality which is madder than any writing made up to amuse and enrage or bore.

I have gleaned from thousands of psychotic episodes in many schools these ghoulish geography teachers who have been to every country but Hell.

Here it is. I teach there.

Barry Dickins
English Teacher

I
The Beginning: Forty Years Ago

I cannot think why I became an English teacher in the grasp for meaning in life's uneven tumbling ground, possibly it was the passion for language in a suburb that didn't have any. My father used to read stories to my brother John and myself out of a lovely 1930 book called *The Children's Treasure House* and they included *Gulliver's Travels* and our Dad would in a completely authentic manner impersonate all the strange characters in Swift's writing as if he knew them all personally.

It was a theatrical household at any rate and my mother wrote to me even when I was in State School at Grade Four level; she had effortless handwriting and without thinking I copied her and have always written personal letters in the exact same script as hers. I was not a strong reader since I used to get distracted so easily because the first sentence or pearly paragraph could be so entrancing I just had to write as well.

I always loved people and talk mixed together and have invariably theatricalised my life to make a good story a better one but then again I have had a problem in that I have always found it just about impossible to separate life from writing or the street from drama or weeping from joking.

I decided to teach English forty years ago exactly in my pursuit of career and wife and to that end I strolled one day I did down ever-leafy Grattan Street Carlton to the Old Melbourne State College where in those days everyone was nicer and more sophisticated. Drivers of large cement mixers didn't run over you back then in Grattan Street but gently waved you under their tyres. The building was ancient and leaved with hope.

The curly balustrades walked you up to fascinating lessons given by men in tweed who read *The Times Literary Supplement* over a nice pipe you as a student were sometimes, if you were good, given a puff of. The carpets were deep like proofreading.

The voices were professorial even in the car park full of eye-watering scooters and depressing German tutors who chewed raw potatoes and knew Bertold Brecht.

I studied thoroughly and passed all my exams except Classroom Management because I suppose I didn't have any authority.

We were sent out on what were called 'rounds', which meant trying to learn just how to teach swarms of rude city children who appeared to have a pathological hatred of all.

No one ever taught us how to teach. Full stop. When I attended the lessons at the old State College nobody on their staff taught us to expect difficulties not to mention tragedies during our own lessons in time to come; there was merely data and the teachers in those days were more concerned with surface appearances such as terrific tits than the psychological fact of kids who can't speak, learn, write or remember.

The old teachers didn't blow dope or get drunk or anything like that but they didn't really think or see things spontaneously. They looked okay but weren't interesting and went to cutting-edge theatre but were more concerned with remembering where they'd parked.

It was all halls that led to more halls and unpleasantness on the telephone. It was soft slamming of noiseless tutorial chambers and lectures you forgot as they were said. You didn't learn a thing in 1970 when I completed my Dip. Ed. But I mean to say I am pleased to have it and it has got me several residencies in schools whenever I've remembered to get it out of my wallet with bits of boiled fruit cake all through it.

In Carlton in my day a steak cost two dollars with fat big chips and salad and they said hello as you flopped down and read pornography or The Phantom.

I recall how we went to my first placement which was Boil Street Special School. I taught there over 40 years ago now I'm back only old but absolutely nothing changes in education.

Soon kids will either shoot up at home or get wiped out on booze and we teachers shall text their grades through to the morgue the way things are going but I may be wrong and I hope I am because I love teaching and wouldn't want to do it dead. Although being deceased it may be easier to do reports. Report writing has killed many an honest teacher. Weekends can be more fraught than school days and that's saying a fair bit.

I still recall my first day here so vivid is my shame and anaesthetised sense of death by ignorance. None of the staff say 'Hi' upon my entrance on that morning when the Education Department sent me to Coventry, or Sickening Road which is twenty miles of Italians and no money. It is ugliness in all its entrancing aspects and perfectly treeless because no tree in its right mind would flower here.

All that flowers is parking fines and discontent.

Upon my first day way back in 1970 when I graduated with my longed-for Diploma Of Education scored at the old Melbourne State College in Carlton I was terribly excited to begin the illumination and opiated wonder of learning. I cut myself then as I still do today three tomato and cheese Tip Top white bread sandwiches and bunged in a pear and took with me *The Best Poems In English For Seven Hundred Years* published by Oxford University Press and sat on the manic-depressive foul open-plan tram crammed full of unemployable English teachers and waited for something fantastic to happen. It did. The tram stopped.

It stopped next door to a big place full of ugly things for the poor. They are today called Savers and fashionable

The Beginning: Forty Years Ago

middle class people browse the putrescence in search of rabies. That day 41 years ago no one spoke to me and I had to do a search for the coffee. It took all day to discover the pantry where the International Roast had its bent teaspoon padlocked to a fine mesh length of chain so it was quite tricky helping oneself as it tended to viciously attack you, even scald you. Then as now no one said anything to you and there was no timetable just as there was no sense.

Boil Street was the oldest, well practically oldest Government-designed State School ever. It was built based on a vision belonging to Governor Gipps, who invented Gippsland amongst other things and the crumbly edifice has stood teetering between the old Melbourne Jail and Sickening Road for two complete centuries. It is of horrid bluestone adzed by manic prisoners fresh off the barges of tetanus and mild scurvy that ferried them over from Great Britain and Ireland to rid the rich of poets. Not merely poets of course but fabric designers and sexually-challenged Welshmen who dreamt of getting hung in Coburg: thousands of demented poor old things set to work by candlelight or burning orb in sky of day to construct the world's most awful jail and they were flogged hard in the doing and in the boredom of it and the penal servitude of time that belongs to Governors because a prison sentence in those treacly days was called 'At The Governor's Pleasure'. The State School System Of Victoria meant that free born children could understand cognitive mind collapse as early at Prep or 'Bubs' which stood for 'Babies', presumably, although it's impossible to presume anything.

Boil Street Educators in days of yore were instructed in only two things. How to whip an infant and how to kill it if it spoke back.

Boil Street teaching men toiled in other trades to supplement a meagre salary and were forced to take on part-time work hacking down hanged newsagents off the scaffold till very late at night and as a consequence didn't get in to have their tea till after eight at night even then it took a fair scrub in the bloodied trough to get the gore off their palms.

Teachers 200-years-ago in Victoria were schooled in Geography mostly and illiteracy. They knew, some of them, where Wonthaggi was, but didn't know what it did or what it meant. They were not fit in the brutal flogging times and often struggled up Sickening Road, suffering from advanced scurvy or even insanity. They flogged their way clear.

The old school where I ended up has no amenities so it rather resembles a Steiner School which doesn't understand 2012 or wool or The World Trade Centre bombardment, which has to be a good thing. The creaky teachers crawl in the creaky doors and teach thousands of internationally poor kids how to count and use English, otherwise, and they know it, they perish for want of knowledge.

The Boilers teach the raw basics without which you stand in front of a tram and get flattened pretty much straight away these days. I am accepted here because I live here. I look exactly like all the others who teach in this dump.

The kids also come from the poorest places on Earth and their brothers and sisters have died for want of Drought Broth. None of the staff boasts a mint-new navy coloured BMW convertible with bucket seats and starlight navigation aids. They mostly catch the tram to work and read the paper and do their best all the day at their beloved place of learning. They offer complimentary bananas to deaf children who go without at home, which very often is a burnt-out car in Moreland somewhere.

None of the teachers eats in front of me, they couldn't as it would be a sin and hurt them. They peel up their Coburg Market Seville Oranges and gladly hand them out to the orange-less.

They are happy and they never go crook about how hard they work, not like the losers at Posh College who are bone lazy, almost too bone lazy to keep steering their sports cars up the road after work, not that they ever do that. They detest learning at Posh because I mean what good does it do you? It's all about your bearing and your clothes from Myers. The desks are out of alignment at Boil Street but the kids are perfectly true and reasonable. They scream at play but kids ought to scream at morning play and scrcam when their black mummies and daddies pick them up for Safaris after the bell sounds at 3.30 pm, deafening as a flower you'd never deign to pick.

I love each nook and bad-tempered temp who dreams of permanency at Reception; I love each curly sandwich and peer into cramped fungussy lockers of kids with delight and see cheap exercise-lined books where the kids strive to write out the English alphabet. The day dissolves in less than a second here and after school we form societies where the kids debate, play darts, wrestle each other and use the exhausted monkey-bars until home comes in sight, even if that is the burnt-out shell of a car not far from the old school where I've landed right on my footsies.

The classrooms are choked but the liberty is wide and hand-spaced. The kids amble in and dance to their own hand-made-music and we actually think and write better when no one's the boss. We're all that.

That afternoon of that first day two of the physical education hulks of six foot each way tall told me they intended to organise an indoor soccer match in the middle of the hall, and did I mind getting my silkscreen gear out the way – I used to teach forgery amongst other subjects – and after a time the Year 7s got adept at printing wonderful five-buck banknotes and I said that was okay for nothing gave me more pleasure than having a hard-pumped vinyl soccer ball booted up my unexpected bottom. I was in the middle of packing up my stuff and prising open lids of ink and jamming lids back on tins of printer's ink when the game began in fearful earnest.

The kids were all tearing around the dusty main circular room kicking the ball with the most tremendous force and nets for goals were improvised and kids were being famous English or Macedonian heroes all over the place and the physical education teacher-hulks were giving them the red card and blowing tin whistles with a yard of slag coming out the end of them and everyone as per usual screaming and swearing and very wildly blaspheming. And after about five minutes as I was packing up my silkscreen stuff a particular player who was illiterate in grade 6 kicked the new ball right into my face and down I went for the count.

I was unconscious upon my first day of teaching silkscreen printing. The blow off the ball burst my nose in two places and I lay unconscious in a vast pool of gore that oddly was black, quite black, and my groggy body was weak as a kitten sniffing glue. They dragged me to the sideline so as not to interrupt the first quarter and nobody checked me or bothered to call an ambulance. Then as now I was flotsam. I was just in their important way. They were soccer stars.

I managed to put some yards of industrial strength toilet paper round my so swollen head then hopped on the tram, blood dripping everywhere. I couldn't seem to clog up any more and wound my own jumper round my own head to keep my nose on because so much of it had been kicked right off it. I paid the surly tram conductor a dollar to go into my city.

I alighted at Princes Bridge and walked a study in scarlet to Prince Henry's Hospital where I walked into Casualty; I was so seriously distracted that I actually pushed the M button for 'Mortuary'.

But no one told me off.

They matter-of-factly set my nose in two places and put plaster over my new nose and handed me some capsules of Aspirin which I gratefully gulped then shook hands with the doctors and went back to work again at about 1pm. When I walked in no one asked me how I was or what the hospital had done for my health. They couldn't have cared less as in their charter which is not to inquire into suffering. Just get on with it.

I noticed my blood had been half-heartedly mopped away in the centre of the main area but my cans of ink were all over the place and pages of paper calling me swear words had been successfully printed on my printing press but by now were all fluttering around the grubby space.

I was asked to teach grammar to Year 6s who called me a swear word as soon as I went in the tiny gagging dormitory room where my bag of books and Tip Top white bread sandwiches were but something had devoured them, possibly a contagion of Sickening Road flying rats: the seagulls.

I went home to my rented room and ran the bath all those years ago and was surprised to learn the water was lovely and boiling-hot for once, possibly because I'd managed to pay the rental. The blood came off me and I lay at my ease in the fantastic hot sudsy water not minding what had happened in the slightest degree. I was reading *The Songs Of Experience* anyway and figured dear old William Blake, he being a teacher too, and a printer and hymn-inventor, would have laughed it off and perhaps written a verse about his similarly unexpected dislocated nose. I fell asleep in my single bed and waited for the alarm clock to call me to teaching at 6am. I dreamt of noses.

But now is now and today is teaching 41 years later in the same shit-hole with the identical teachers I collided with when I was so youthful and so starry-eyed as in the Genesis, my favourite writing. I wanted to be either a kindergarten teacher or a minister carrying the word of love when I was young, but I enjoyed my teacher-rounds as they are called in your three-year course at college and have become what I always was. Lost.

Now the kids grumble and lizard into my dorm room with Simon who is their main English guy; they throw their heavy backpacks so they either hit other kids in the body to the salute of 'Yes!' Or else these bags of Coke and textbooks that weigh several kilos easily hit the filthy floor where they lie unstudied. The kids all appear thirty and have ghoulish faces like unhappy ghosts who couldn't really care if the sky fell on Sickening Road. It should and then there would be no teaching.

As I gazed at boy or girl or whatever they are, with the cunning in them that refuses all help and the narcissism in them that conquers all pity, my mind travelled back to my old State School which happened to be Keon Park next door to Thomastown where I loved going to school so much I honestly used to run to it: run through those sun-dappled lanes, dodging errant chickens pecking away at their numeracy, hurling my young frame through geranium hedges, making daisy chains for my first girlfriend Helen Waxell, and then to write with my teachers first letters of heavenly literacy that all formed the word Love.

I loved reading and writing when I was a child but look at these sullen masturbators! I look up at them and their mouths resemble cut slots in a tin money box! Foolishly perhaps I say 'Hi!' The universe indeed is equally divided into the halves. The people who say hi and the people who never do. I said hi when my Mum had me and she said hi back.

Now she's so ill and enfeebled but still says hi with her beautiful old eyes at me when I come in once a week to see them at the old home.

The pupil-ogres hate me and all chorus 'Fuck you you fat pig!' when I smile wearily at them. Today we are to compose theatre dialogue for the school review and unluckily for me one of my heart condition pills is causing me bladder woes deep within, and I urgently need to go again.

I excuse myself to Simon and explain my problem and he shrugs and says 'Go to it!' I stumble out towards the rubble and the chaos of the courtyard because I'm absolutely bursting but as per usual both staff brick toilets are multi-secured with vast lumps of chain and thick heart-breaking brass padlocks that seem a yard big. Kids who are at recess are drolly lolling about in the squished exercise area smoking or joking; others of them are setting fire to a trapped dove in a waste paper bin and then igniting it with a Bic lighter.

I again am required to wee on my boots because it is below zero by six degrees and possibly it is the en masse screaming that is making me go so much, it's hard to say really. The screaming for no reason mixed with the shrieking of supersonic tram brakes is pretty hard to deal with unless one is deaf, which I nearly am. I go upstairs again up the choking dusty stairs with 1969 grass matting glued to it dangerously so that you tend to trip over it all the time on your way to teach.

For some inexplicable reason volcanic ash there was certainly in the dorm room; it has to have drifted into and over Australia from Chile or somewhere insanely volcanic. I examined my boots and saw volcanic ash so hot on them it must have just erupted. Brian Epstein the principal has just come in the room and told me in my ear I can work another year here if I like. 'Fuck', I intoned without thinking. Thinking is the enemy of the people.

The other drones mumble and stuff round with no intention of doing any work. They are hooded nong-nuts.

One big fat ghastly boy is thirty stone in weight with wary eyes that have nothing behind them named Tex. He is writing a film script upon vampires possibly because he's one of them. His gigantic rolypoly fingers squatly type rapidly and rabidly and he blasphemes at every chance as he writes the most vile thing ever recorded in English. He informs it happens to be his birthday but when I foolishly wish him a happy one he curses me face to face.

I look up and down at the twelve hooded pupils who resemble freshly laid hot asphalt just glowing with seething resentment. They are a raiment of hate.

They loathe sweetness and only love and respect Coke or the repellent sugar-hit doughnuts over the road or synthetic apple pies bedaubed with false whipped cream. They guts into these as they chainsmoke before school starts again like a coagulated lung somehow starting again. How do I teach them anything?

When I did my Dip. Ed. no one taught my year how to stand in front of kids and interest them. At one Community School a girl in my year killed herself because she saw herself as a failure who didn't have the foggiest clue about teaching highrise sugar freaks who have the attention span of a gnat. And an Aboriginal girl was found hanged in the girl's loo by our cleaner. I felt sorry for him.

I am now alone with two bad boys I can't interest in any way shape or form, the first of whom is engaged in the deed of using a thieved Philips Head green screwdriver to gouge out of the main brick wall a gigantic double-house brick that would come in at a hundred pounds in weight. He couldn't care less that I am teaching drama. He contentedly, patiently digs out the dirty big heavy double brick piecemeal and that is his double English lesson for today. To dig out a big brick then drop it out the church window right on someone's head.

I try and look to Simon to show with my frightened eyes, the facial expression of alarm because I actually have a pupil's temporary attention and don't want to lose it much after an hour of nothing doing. Simon is saying to the boys in general 'You can swear if you like but only if it's in context.' The boys dry hump one another as the girls screw up paper with my plot outlines written on them and pop them out the window whereupon they kill flying geese.

The determined nonchalant youth covered in acne, malnourished son of an unemployed smack freak who used to attend Boil Street now has unearthed the old heavy bricks joined together with very thick plaster and Victorian era cement and in a most relaxed manner crosses leisurely to the freezing open window that looks down 50 foot right over the footpath and raises it to brain someone with it. But I stop him doing it and he looks all vulnerable and crushed, poor thing!

'I know what you intend to do with that double brick and I'm not letting you do it!' I couldn't really believe my own language. I was talking pure Sickening Road. He resisted me for a time, brief was that time when my brawny arm stopped murder by him, but even then I was very strong, as in my whole physical family are all very strong when push comes to shove. I glared at him and my 1979 dentures they grated at him, the little prick!

He eventually put the old double brick back into its hole in the wall and then went into a decline somewhat, and sort of produced gargling effects into the pencil grooves on that awful cheap desk of his. It commences to rain as it can only rain in Sickening Road, a desultory manner that soaks even the temporary meaning out of cheap tasteless rockbuns. I look down from my eyrie and a dog appears to be masturbating, a man is pulling his wife's hair out of her head in large painful tufts just because he's in Sickening Road and she seems to approve for she does not desist.

The lad who gouged so workman-like the great heavy bricks out of our main wall remains hypnotically in the retina of my memory-eye. Is he the uneducated youth of today, personified in elementary rebellion and doomed to sloth through each wasted school day saying 'I'm not doin' this shit!' He came across to me just before when I pulled that brick-thing out of his nerveless grasp and he made a point of ramming the Philips Head screwdriver right in my old face, as though to say 'Do you want this in your head?' I didn't much as it turned out.

I pulled the weapon from him and placed it by our much-scuffed and kicked-in door, a vast thump sound it produced that made the anaemic children feebly scream. The sinning boy folded his scrawny arms in defiance and glared my way and then said to me, 'Who's to stop me doin' what I fucking like?' Well, yes, exactly. That's right. Who here at Boil Street is to stop you being a fool?

I managed to get through in my way via sheer persistence and much pleading to a few malnourished Year 5 children and to my general surprise they joined in with me for over an hour. We wrote about the fate of animals and I developed the theme of pity where creatures were concerned. Would you save a run-over dog in the middle of Moreland Road, clocked by the bus with its tongue hanging out or would you take it somehow to the Lort Smith Animal Hospital in North Melbourne and save it? Or would its agonising death be hilarious?

The authors wrote really well-argued dialogues and we then shared which we used to call reading aloud. The cultural cringe exists all right and Americanisms clog our speech and original writing so much so I heard a young woman teacher at our Monday Morning Conference refer to a sand castle as play-equipment.

The little street-kid authors very shyly read their lines back to the group, even acted it out and included car back-firing effects and used improvisatory words to great effect, I have to say here in my memoirs, because I do not lie and agree with the truth in every degree, setting down on these memory pages the chaos and oddities and marvels of child genius writers I've worked with all my life in the dorm-room in Sickening Road.

Simon was doing much better than me. He had the inspiration of getting the Year 5s to act out their lines of dialogue to a camera within his great big modern video and then playing it back. The kids were silenced and enraptured all at once because they saw in a fraction of a second that they were gifted, not just as actors who had the skills to fetch life to words they'd just written but to see their very own movie. When Simon beamed in his grizzly way and told them 'See, it isn't that hard, is it?' they cheered.

So all of a sudden we had the moment and we had momentum.

The kids became keen as mustard on living language

and because they have grown up dodging trams and leaping before cement mixers and being hassled by police and going to school starving-hungry and putting up with junkie and alcoholic single parents the idea of writing for the screen was realised by them in one fell swoop. It was great of course to hear anything cheer in Boil Street.

Simon collected the original scrawling on butcher paper donated by the butcher over the road and we both filed it away in a folder after the kids had managed to type it up. Simon gave me such a smile of the breakthrough it really was to see the kids take to writing, but just as they packed up which means kicking their vile bags through the door. I stupidly inquired of them if they'd like me to help them correct their English after morning play. One of them swore at me with half-eaten hot dog rotating within his be-furred teeth, surely a break-through sight in my life, so that I heard and saw 'Get fucked you great big faggot cunt!'

But never mind. It really had been a big breakthrough to get a fraction of English actually written out and then see how happy there were for some infinitesimal moment of longing to write your thoughts then see them acted out. I looked at the latest staff conference with them all eagerly but unemotionally emailing their contexts to each other at a wall of new computers that the federal government shouted them to help celebrate learning since The First Fleet moored off Sickening Road.

Now it is another fatal Monday and the team at Boil Street are talking low and intently about sexual harassment in Prep.

'It is okay to say no!' badges that have come in from Office Works are being sold to the stoned parents of all Preps for two bucks a piece; some of the parents are so out of it they put them on themselves, although it's tough to find room for a pin-hole on their skinny bodies.

The shy Preps are summoned in and the filthy hall lights are put out and a movie is shown depicting anal intercourse with q&a afterward.

'Any questions children of Prep E?' croons Brian taking a squint at the Danish slides that accompany the kit from Vic Ed.

'Does it hurt getting fucked up the arse?' asks a nice Prep but Brian isn't sure how to answer that one.

'Only at first,' puts in a teacher, but Brain shushes him violently.

'Today we are facing a sexual crisis in Sickening Road of unbelievable proportions,' says Brian gravely. 'People today want sexual gratification even in Balwyn. Turtles are pregnant on every branch.'

Kids develop thrush just thinking about pavements and you can get pregnant without a charge on the Puffing Billy with a Thai national who may offer you a lolly to please him in Belgrave or under some sort of tunnel with no undergarments on. The problem today is that Spring has come.

And we with it even if we don't want to. My wife came this morning because I've put in a brand new Roll-A-Door. But it's all right to say no, just remember that Preppies Of Boil Street. Before you run off with a Black.

The Preps then ran out to Morning Play and I supervised them going the grope. It was refreshing frankly to see so many of them use the monkey bars with no pants on. Brian got a barbecue going but the ferocious smoke stung the Preps' eyes so some had to go home ill.

I have been asked to go on camp tomorrow with the Year Elevens to Inverloch so that'll be a bit of a change from English.

It was hard in a way to see where the Preps might fit into our society after Boil Street had done with them.

The School Camp

Camp came and a torrid fortnight it was at Inverloch with leaky tents with six kids in each of them and a cabin for teachers with all these hard morose beds with no support. There was little in the way of heating and most nights the team lay on each other to keep the chilblains out, not that I get them, but a lot did and they can be very hurtful if they are not acted on.

I slept out in the open in a grotty sleeping bag. I adore the stars and know some of them shall look after me and there were plenty of them to be sure on the beach at Inverloch which is the Aboriginal for Inverloch.

Breakfast was a hearty look-round.

The kids loved the sea-change and at first hurt each other less. In the city they are victims of tram-rage and every other form of anger that is inevitable given what torments the traffic offers.

It was wondrous and never to say revolutionary to stroll along a real beach and build a sand castle or just run in the free breeze that brought with it such liberty instead of gorging up the diesel fumes of endless semi trailers that choke fun to death all along the strip outside the stripped school that is leached of frivolity, not so much the light heartedness that often the most stressed pupil finds in his day or his desk, but the teachers who are so glued to modern stress in all its forms, from striving to keep up with emails and trying to scream down streaming cooped-up kids who are sick of themselves as well as their overseers.

The sea wind dresses your soul differently; it understands you better than the city, with all its cut-price hysterias and tenth-rate charms such as the latest sugar-hits emblazoned upon billboards to indoctrinate mindless consumers in the arts of survival known as chocolate, wine, Panadol or Death.

The kids you could see let what was left of their hair down on the common beach of latter day hope or surf; it was perfectly delightful to sit around a log fire at night on the sand and just for once try to get through an Uncle Scrooge comic. You found you had time for them at Inverloch and enjoyed their company in deference to their non-contribution at school.

The next school camp took place at The Boilies which is a terrible coastal error near Warrnambool where waves can prove fatal just looking at them. I got on really well with the young suave staff and, although I was nowhere as sleek or fit as them and couldn't swim, I really enjoyed the whole novel experience.

We rigged up vast tents in no time right on the tip of the yawning cliff and hit in the spikes with a really good satisfying thump. The wind was picking up a bit but the girls and guys I was with swore it wasn't a fuss. I agreed with them that I loathed fuss.

It rained and howled like several banshees that first night of the outing and it was hard to cook things for the kids in such trying conditions, but we got hot dogs happening, thousands of them without any bursting their skins because a lot of skinny under-nourished kids hate sausages that have even slightly ruptured and won't come at them. I was in charge of food and apart from serving up hot-dog coloured Bushells tea using frankfurt water I was mistake-free.

The rolls they liked, the rolls they chomped and about fifty kids blew over the cliff but it really didn't matter much since we found most of them again in the morning, even though the weather was worse, worse than worse, rather like the end of the world.

It was a long night though, of sopping wet sleeping bags, wet and dry humping, Koori kids disappearing and most of us forgetting to do a head count. We didn't have a telephone so none of us could get in touch with police or the school so far away. The art teacher one night drew pictures in the campfire ash of prehistoric beasts and one of the kids screamed because it was too realistic.

We had a few swinging kerosene lamps attached or sort of attached to the unpredictable ceiling that didn't exist on the top bit of my big saggy and blowy tent so the kids could have a brief read of their pornography or history of Rome or whatever it was. I read *Treasure Island* to lots of kids until I couldn't do it any more. You get sick and tired of pirates on camp, you really do.

Late on the second night a boy near me kept whispering about how sensitive I was and then he started to feel my leg, the left one. I didn't know what to do about him so I read poetry to him until he yawned so powerfully he fell asleep on his still wet all rucked-up sleeping bag. I read my gas account and went to sleep still clutching it. About an hour later he was standing over me with a stiffy.

Somehow I got through the long evening in the tent but awoke completely shagged although he didn't bugger me, which of course would have made his report a bit harder.

The rest of the holiday was a nightmare of trying to shoo away dying seals that stunk a fair bit as they lay dying on us all the time. No teacher ought to smell a dying seal. Not once. The weather was inclement; the kids were bored; the seals did not end.

One day walking along what I think is called a bit of headland I spied a sulphuric seal barking its brains out on a rock. I went near it to try to soothe it, placate it as it was coughing so melodramatically and plaintively and probably emphysemically. I put my friendly right hand near its suffering and the fool of a thing tried to bite it off. Its poor old mouth was gagging all this dreary detergent muck all the time as though some how it had been munching Omo. Its demented barking sounded exactly like the kids. I nearly asked it to get out its pencil case and rule up its margin.

The kids got into the big van and we chugged back to town which took five hours because we ran over a bolt in Dandenong. Some got van-sick and vomited forlornly all the way home but others of them read books or tried sex every time we turned left.

They were supposed to do a project on the sea camp and some did drawings from memory of the fucking seals. Others didn't remember a single event as there weren't any apart from drowning. A girl did drown one day but no one liked her. She eventually recovered, someone said and the death was vilely exaggerated.

A few days later I dropped over to the parents of the boy who'd tried hard to hurt me and they made a delicious cup of tea and in a friendly manner they served up roly-poly cake. We sat in their luxuriant sitting room stirring tea and nibbling cake that was just so fresh it felt a sad shame to eat it.

I didn't really know how to begin dobbing in their perfectly normal, if rabid, son. I lied to begin with badly and said he was an excellent boy who always strove to learn at his school but they contradicted this and said he was just dreadful in every way, shape or form.

'We'd like him hanged,' said his mother, passing the delicious roly-poly cake.

'ASAP,' added his father. And they meant it.

'We're are not shocked that he tried to hurt you as he's often attempted it on us,' his Mum said, sipping her hot tea very powerfully like a suction-thing. 'Some children oughtn't to be conceived or born,' added his polite Mum. 'They disappoint and enrage from the day they enter their playpen.'

The father told me I did the right thing when I throttled him in the camp-tent; but I always felt a bit bad about that and thought perhaps I'd over-reacted, but then again I'd never been hurt like this before.

'No, he's just shit!' declared his father, chomping into the last crumb of cake with a look of hate.

'Just perfect shit!' agreed his mother who spat hard on the cake dish then scooped up all the things and cast them in the sink in the kitchen.

When I left they both said simultaneously 'Why do you bother with him?'

The eternal problem of trams up Sickening Road addresses my wits today during the last day of school holidays and I must point out that trams like suicide have no meaning. It is terribly cruel of course for a teacher to murder himself due to upsetting lateness of Coburg trams: what other reason can there possibly be? But ever remember suicide is illegal and one can be charged for it and even placed in a lock-up.

Being shoved nose-first in a lock-up is no different from, spiritually, purchasing an adult tram ticket to get you in roughly one piece from Moreland Road Brunswick to Boil Street Coburg North, true intersection of Heaven And Hell.

Designed in Purgatory by brain dead rocket scientists with a nod to Werner Von Braun the Nazi who went on to design both the Blitz Bomb as well as Disneyland, the first verifiable public death upon a Sickening Road tram car came about in 1972, the day I started teaching class at Boil Street. I know that for a fact because I was on it when the guy opposite me dropped dead of ugliness when he got on.

He didn't look too crash-hot to me the nervy way he alighted with both alacrity and advanced paranormal paranoia; fair enough he realised he was dead meat the second it shuddered to a timeless halt at Moreland Road. It was raining buckets down the foul necks of unwashed Greeks as they swore in their own tongue and carted like mules their hideous painted plywood trolleys full of dirty big spuds – god almighty Greeks eat a lot of them.

They all resembled unintelligent Zorba The Greeks as they bit each other to get on. They wore tiresome goatherd trousers lined with Greek newspapers to keep the cold at bay; strive as they may that proved difficult because it was pretty hard to buy a copy of a newspaper they could read and remember in Brunswick. But line their bottoms with newspapers they did since it was the only thing the poor things could think of in 2 degree heat even in early October.

The goatherd mentality is very strong in Sickening Road and Greek men seem in cold times to will the tram to come. They stand there freezing and swearing in pure unadulterated goatherd and mentally force the even colder tin tram to appear up Sickening Road like a metal mirage full of flu and bronchitis and plenty of scrumptious allergies that float toxic up from divine asphalt and concrete drains like the scourge of all lifehay fever.

The hay-fevered Greeks sneeze all over their saturated tickets and blow their noses on their women as soon as they get on and it starts shuddering and hesitating and the prong comes off the roof and then the driver gets the prong back on and everyone on board is either blank of countenance or weeping for the old country which is even worse an experience than Coburg.

Hundreds of Italians plucking bantams with no heating on it, blood and bantam feathers on the turn-off to Albion Street, but sadly the driver keeps ever onward steering The Black Hole Of Calcutta towards Boil Street where a few desultory guests of pneumonia hop off swearing and casting remnants of beheaded chickens all over the foot-deep puddles on the awful pitiless road of no hope. Worse than Athens in hundred degree heat. Worse than Rome with an earache.

The women all gnaw bunches of garlic and slag out the pith on the slats of the tram car floor where kids try to dig out filthy chewies from between the slats that tram designers dreamt up to benefit public traction. The women are all widows with chin beards and no sex memory. They all wear black cardigans and work 100-hour shifts at garment factories run by their grandfathers or uncles. The men smoke hand-rolled thick vile acrid eye watering obscene cigarettes that blind and nauseate others on the tram who don't smoke because they don't want to die that way.

The driver of the tram drinks home-made alcohol out of a bottle from the Old Country with a brown paper bag twisted round it and he smokes too and mutters Moreland Road to himself like a litany as he tried hard to see Boil Street which is a thing of meaning like lung or throat cancer only it doesn't jump around in you.

The conductor of the tram pokes people in the testicles with her iron-framed money and ticket bag and salty coins tumble into it with sticky fingered regret because life is hard and trams are awful and you shouldn't need to pay for them.

People treat the idiotic tram ride as meal-break time and saw up a pineapple with a bread knife they keep up their leg just in case and people suck the acidic juice through the repellent zig-zag husks and chuck the waste on the filthy slippery floor. People are so crude they do just any old thing they feel like and some try hard to come on to others and others try to press a sex organ onto a Carlton Football Club supporter, not that they'd ever suspect anything anyway. Turkish grandmothers gobble turnips and spit through the open doorway at Greek pedestrians who just stand on Sickening Road in the wet because they forgot to wave their arm for the tram in the first instance.

The moral imperative on any tram is to feel worse, how worse is entirely up to each doomed passenger fool enough to get on one of them. As a young and trusting eager teacher who had just started at the old hall I didn't have a car, couldn't possibly afford one anyway and just waited for one of them to gulp me up after work and bear me home to die of shaking.

I just had my essays to correct and poems by kids to read at home, that sort of stuff and try as I might I couldn't try and read a single thing on the jolting conveyance that kicked and bucked and bronco'd and hissed and mechanically belched and I collided with suicidal conductors with their great bags thrust round their gut and one night after work I saw this exhausted tram driver guy all red in the face just lose it and cast his entire ticket and change harness bag into the Moreland Road intersection because he'd had trams full stop!

The instant the silver and heavy copper change landed on the wet and bulging road you saw hundreds of starving kids leap for a bit of rare shrapnel and pluck a bit up and bite it to see it was any good to them and then make a bee-line to the burger shop for one with the lot, first proper hot feed they'd scored in a month of Sundays.

Packed is best and packed in like claustrophobic sardines is how it always was with bits of hair on your mouth it was so crushed and intimate; someone's leg in your calf; someone raping you with an umbrella in the rainy open doorway; dogs so skinny they got on for nothing invisibly and comically and operatically and yowled for human kindness and more importantly, food, both sources outsourced in tough times like these times I am talking about on trams that should never have been designed.

And the tram ride is never over. You alight at Boil Street forever and ever. I teach in eternity and have done so for over forty years of horrid tram journeys that only get much worse; today for instance the contemporary passenger plays Satanic music inside her ear cams and the drivers are carefully drugged by unions not to pull up. I have seen many harried people charge along the road after the tram has belted off at rocket speed just because the driver couldn't care less about stopping for an exhausted traveller; their nemesis.

Ten tired teachers from work hop off at bloody Boil Street with me in pouring filthy rain. We don't look at each other on the tram just as never do at school. There's no rapport. We walk until we part at the Coles Supermarket where we shop for chop and salad specials for teachers. They all look much younger than I do and they are much younger and possibly kinder, although I like being spontaneously kind. It's the one thing money can't buy like the cure for gloominess.

I didn't eat last night because my stomach was filled with memories of the Sickening Road tram to Boil Street. Even in my bed I unexpectedly lurched.

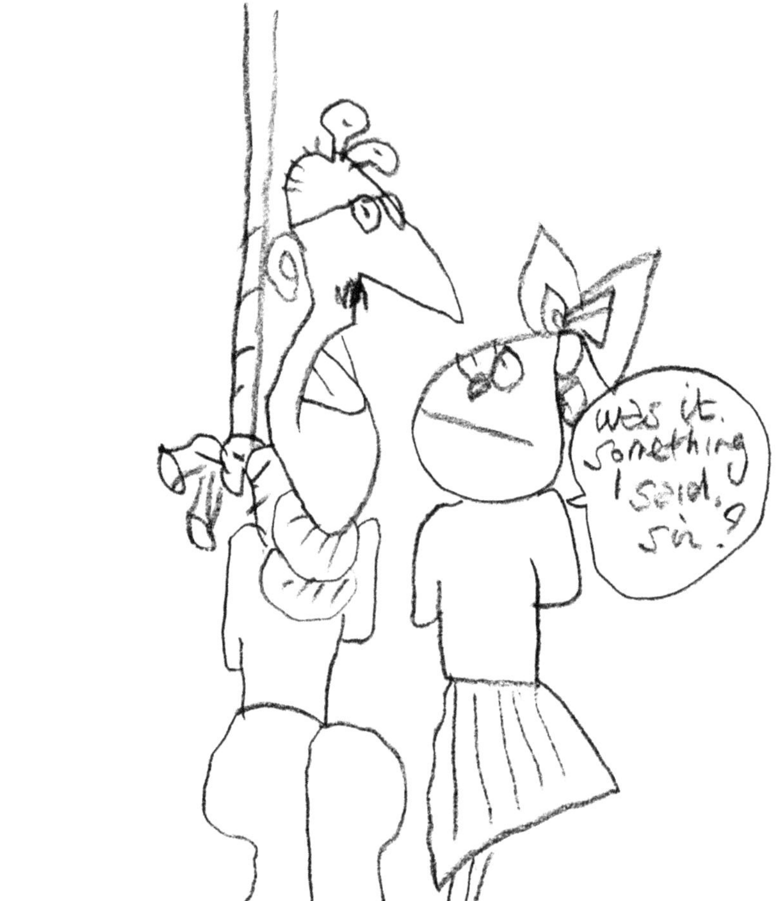
was it something I said, Sir?
16-12-12
Barry Dickins

The Mountain Country

I taught in the Mountain Country after that because as long as I passed my 'Rounds' during my first year it didn't really matter much what school I went to. The mountains were to live for so up them I walked until I turned up one stunning day in April and met the jovial principal Stan Ives who ran Myrtle Primary School on the Myrtle-Aniseed Road.

Sheep were contentedly bleating and healthy and emaciated children were playing soccer and booting an old scuffed football, little girls who'd weigh twenty grams and little boys you could just imagine being lifted up by wedgetail eagles then flown to their lairs for afternoon tea – Heaven Forbid!

I was just the guest for one week but it was heaven to just be with the kids up in the bush. The policy of the small school was the motto of its leader and that is, as I have heard him say to the pupils on Monday Morning Assembly: 'You must remember that you are not here for yourself and to take therefore whatever you can get away with from us but instead you are here for others than you. If a kid, fellow kids experiences a difficulty getting their wheelchair through a puddle or some mud, you must see that as your chance to help and you must help them get to their lesson on time. Lift them up the wet steps and get all the mud out of the clogged-up spokes of their wheels on that instrument that they need to get around with.'

Many times in the course of that country week I witnessed kids eager to lift one or two other kids up through the mud and slush to edge their wheelchair into class, all done unsarcastically remembering their hardworking leader's words about not being there just for themselves only.

I saw parents fetch just-picked fruit from their farms and plonk it down on fresh-rinsed plates done by the Grade Twos using tea towels and not loo paper.

I showed them drawing and poetry and one afternoon we executed caricatures of their dads for Fathers Day cards they made themselves. I sat myself with arms folded so the kids could make cruel caricatures of me: big red nose like Santa, big baggy eyes from chronic hay fever perpetually-pot gut from not exercising enough and too much grog. They drew the lot in no time and I was the first to laugh and purchase them as I intended to start up a gallery just for kids in the city.

The sincerity of that bush school so far from the city transformed my concept of teaching into a philosophy of life. We are not here for ourselves but for love of others even if they are awful.

I loved at lunchtime to see Angela and the other teachers heat up fresh lasagna donated at eleven o'clock that very day by parents, often as not coming a long way across all the paddocks of sheep and other things that just stare at you as they guzzle barbed wire.

The parents do a fruit drive once a week and lay out stunning fresh pickings just for the kids as soon as they enter the school. To me that is Holy Communion, except it's strawberries.

I fell in love with the simple community lesson in humility that we are here to take care of each other as if we all matter more than stuff. Cars are shit and possessions are meaningless. It's all in the gift of un-snooty giving that we're properly educated I think.

I stayed with the Ives and got up early and ate their early morning chook's googs. I thanked them after the week of bush teaching and Mary Ives ran after the train at Aniseed station to hand me three-dozen fresh bantam eggs with straw in the cartons to take back to Melbourne with me. I had to reach out of the moving train doorway to clutch at the eggs and call thanks through the noisy diesel engine.

'You can't head back home without these,' she laughed and panted along the gravel platform. That kind of kindness doesn't happen in the city much.

I suppose, in fact I know, that I fell head over heels with bush teaching after that and her running the way she did along the rough gravel platform with the yummy eggs with the fresh straw creeping under the boxes of them signalled new life and a prejudice towards bush children.

Types of caption: "I'm not doin' this shit!"

II

The More-or-Less Present

One day a great many schools ago now a strange letter whisked into my box and defied the starved molluscs who live in there, who proof-read my domestic accounts before chomping into them, and this funny note proved to be a godsend. It was addressed to me personally and came from the chairman of the Board Of Lost Dogs. I sipped my thoughtful tea over the kitchen table and focused properly with my pince-nez.

The folk at the home for abandoned beagles wished me to come to their annual conference and perhaps speak on the subject of abandonment. They had read articles I'd composed for mass circulation newspapers and magazines that had to do with lost kittens and mixed-up canines because I suppose as an author in Australia I probably identified with them.

I arrived nice and bathed and my hair parted correctly and with my speaking voice warmed and ready to give my address. The premises was stuffed full of men who really looked more dog than chap and ladies who seemed more bitch than secretary. I half expected the men to bay at one stage of proceedings since they resembled mastiffs so uncannily.

The room was ancient and lined with many parched volumes dedicated to the preservation of pets; as well as that I looked up and viewed lots of water colour portraits of poodles and spaniels as well as plaintive and water-logged kittens drowning in rivers.

A trust had been set up for the betterment of children's education by some philanthropic woman with more money than kelpies. It was a staggering sum to be certain and this kind spirit feared for the futures of lost creatures and had seen in her life, a long life it was to be sure, hundreds of whipped German Shepherds and strangled goldfish and poisoned tom cats and made the money available to the animal shelter so that school children, especially in the bush, could possibly write compassionately about the poor things.

I was the candidate as the board felt I had insight into suffering being a poet for my daily nibble at dusk. The fact that I passed my Diploma of Education so was ready, willing and able to go into country schools hitherto unvisited by writers such as I. I stood up and declared my love of pets and remembered my family's list of lazy dogs and docile moggies and spoke tenderly of the fate of creatures under Man.

All this is a long time ago I remember but at the cups of tea and dog food later I felt I had made a very shrewd career move. I joked and sobbed in the company of people who preferred pets to people, with good reason

I might add, because no pet I ever knew left me like a married lady might.

In the morning I caught the bus to mountain country and with my letter of introduction taught sweet bush kids how to rhyme and compose a sonnet on the topic of looking after your goat or sheep or trying to establish a rapport with the estranged family ferret.

I was billeted by terribly friendly school principals who raised sheep and bore children who usually became teachers too; as well as that they helped Mum and Dad in with the chaff and constructed that silo. I was made more welcome than at my old home and often felt more loved than before in the vile city I came from.

I felt I was a boy from the bush and enjoyed the company I discovered in cramped classrooms in old bluestone edifices that invariably had a sepia portrait of Queen Victoria over the fireplace as well as a huge sad placard carved out of strange ugly wood that bore the names of the local bush blokes who perished courtesy of King And Country during The War To End All Wars 1914-1918.

The people I taught with are nothing like city teachers in that they know who is broke on the run-down farm and think nothing of running across miles of parched thistles to give them a feed or just hang out with them and listen to their woes. They don't text.

So it has stood me in good stead that funny-looking envelope that slid into my brick letter-box 40-odd years back. Every Easter I go back to the mountains to teach poetry and drawing to children who never see an artist like me, but speak to me exactly the way they address a sheep, cow, bull or windmill or Principal.

Often as not these tiny schools get closed down by the Education Department or refurbished until they have no history in them.

At one particular little bush school I met a girl in Prep who could effortlessly imitate every bird in the district just perfectly. She and I sat on the sea-saw whilst she shut her young and impressionable eyes and took off the wind as well. She could do the breezes around the playground.

Teaching is boring or miraculous simultaneously at times but for me my prejudice is in the mere listening to country school children who may not be high achievers like their city opposites but can produce creek sounds at the drop of a hat.

Blueberry Primary

My favourite Primary School teacher is Miss Rose whom I met at Blueberry Primary School near Gravelside in the centre of Nowhere. Gravelside is where they hold an eel race once a year and that is all that is known of Gravelside.

Miss Rose is a hive of supersonic energy she receives directly from the souls and spirits of the Preppies she knows so well she would bow her noble head and weep if she should forget one of their birthdays. She knows their dreams and has memorised their fragmented nightmares. She wakes only to hear their sandals running to school through leafy lanes, smoky back streets paved with coloured exercise books they dropped yesterday as they tore after chooks.

Miss Rose bows her body to curtsy to her miniature charges and the bow is reciprocated. The cherubs bubble in and immediately squat on the floor and clasp chubby or skinny palms together in a swift and zig-zag manner like leaves cross-hatched. There would have to be thirty-six kids out the front but she has time for them all and allows each infant a minute to give a fairly accurate account of what they're up to. 'What are you up to dear Robin?' she asks of a poppet with fresh bows in her silky plaits.

'Well, at four-and-a-half I'm not up to much', the child intones and Miss Rose smiles enigmatically.

The kids speak of their ponies mostly and what their chickens had for tea.

Miss Rose is married to the local policeman who once was invited to give a prepared talk on accident prevention but had his spleen ruptured on his way to school and had to cancel from Mortlake Hospital.

Many infants speak indefatigably so Miss Rose hurries them into me.

I am her guest for a month and teach drawing with its companion the black lead pencil and its other friend the sheet of cheapest possible butcher paper, donated by the butcher. Miss Rose and two pretty and two plain monitors hand out the gusty paper as it is humid today accompanied by a sort of hot squall-thing that puts the kids' nerves on end.

They sit up nice and straight and follow me step by step on the blackboard out the front. I draw ducks and so do they. I draw chicks stepping confidently out of their cartoon shells. The children's sweaty arms cling like magnets to their pages as we draw dogs chasing roosters and the splendid sun coming up in the drawn morning; some kids add coloured pencils and introduce flowers and picket fences and grouchy crows and petulant pigs and entire barnyard scenes that attenuate and embroider what once was a circle on butcher paper and no more than that.

They share without arguing and come to me to sharpen a blunt pencil and they joke confidently and add watercolour brushes dipped in red and blue to make things jump. The day went swimmingly of its own accord according to the tried and true plan of Beauty.

Miss Rose personally lifted up Ruthie's wheelchair and almost tripped she did with the weight of child and chair and with her forehead bespattered with perspiration she sort of corrected the imbalance and got Ruthie upright again in the room where we were to compose poems on Life And Nothing Else But. Miss Rose invented that title by the way.

Ruthie caterwauled and sobbed anguished biting her saturated hankie just like one of the weeping women by Picasso. She wriggled and sniggled and snickered and jolted and jerked and leapt and whirled and unfurled with the mysterious disease in her body driving all the spasms. The kids of Miss Rose all knew Ruthie since her birth; nothing very much surprised them where their crooked classmate was concerned. They knew her condition off by heart and spoon-fed her custard that Miss Rose' policeman husband had made the night before because he knew Ruthie loved custard.

I loved to see the kids crouch round Ruthie's wheelchair, grasping its muddy tyres, gesticulating to the seemingly impossible child, but no they got through to her who was writhing within her spectral seat. They communicated, they drew her as caricature and she was given a big pen that worked and manufactured a decent thick dark line on her butcher paper and she was assisted, they assisted their sick classmate and one put cardboard upon his back to support Ruthie's butcher's paper and Ruthie drew a cat and all the kids said it was just like one.

At Morning Play I saw Miss Rose pushing the wheelchair around the back of the goal posts of the football oval, a shortened variation of one, and I saw the magpies try to peck Miss Rose's multigrain salad roll and to no avail did they go at it for Miss Rose gobbled it and she helped Ruthie to sort of eat her roll as they trundled round the green rain-soaked ground together, with the girl screaming louder than crow-calls and with even less meaning, then the kids helped her in again and we all wrote a poem about The Love Of The Other.

After school Miss Rose helped all the kids onto the bus to Aniseed and made sure they hadn't forgotten their bags. She waved goodbye to Ruthie's mother after getting her in the car which was full of rust and didn't have a passenger side door, luckily, so Ruthie was easier to get in. Then we waved to them both and the old bomb car rattled and groaned and slid in mud all the way through the path between the big old pine trees behind Blueberry Primary.

There was no cleaner so Miss Rose swept up the trash and bent to pluck up discarded and very lethal brown and black greasy discarded banana peels chucked under the warped grey tin lockers that smelt like hot coloured pencils and glued erasers stuck hard to laughter.

I sat with a pooped Miss Rose after the bus and she wiped the honesty off her skinny arms in her jumper and said she needed a replacement, or at least she needed a rest and then I asked her the prognosis on Ruthie and she didn't say anything but just looked death at me and I left it at that.

On my way home on the suffocating train I thought of Ruthie in her gesticulating wheelchair and the hordes of kids surrounding her, all of them talking animatedly together and the beautiful white face of the girl who is to die since there's no known cure for what ails her; poor thing she is. 'Medical science can only look away in her case,' said Miss Rose as she put the mop and broom away then locked up, making sure the fridge was running because parents had put a pav in. I worked at Blueberry for a week then taught at Posh.

Posh College

A year ago Posh College wrote to me care of my slum in North Coburg stating their desire to have me teach prose to their impressive Year Elevens whom they called 'Sevens' as in 7 Eleven junkfood outlets. Indeed their school magazine was called 'Sevens'. The letter was impressively formed with fountain pen with loops and scrolls in the main text and the paper was of onion, as in onion paper that I think Captain Cook wrote with since it was far cheaper to post onion paper than be hooked with over the top charges for writing on stiff kelp or even cardboard which takes ages to grow in some rainforest somehow.

The Principal at Posh shook me savagely as I was ushered into his vast chandelier'd rooms. His mortarboard fell off he was that excited and stooped he did to bend his back and front and both sides in order to pick it up again, which he did using a compass and groaning. His body was old but fat and firm and I guess you'd call him fat but fit. Any way he ushered me over to his 1740 oak desk and flounced his cape over his shoulders in the manner of master at Eton. I watched his heavy well-oiled shoes murder a big bug under his desk as he squeezed a bell that electronically summoned an ugly lady with tremendous coffee straight out of nowhere. She left the jug of delicious percolated drink on the desk where it made a vile ring on the Principal's neat stack of just-printed letterheads and envelopes bearing the famed school's crest with hard to follow Latin under it. He frowned and the lady shit herself.

'Where do you live Dickins?' he smiled as he stirred his beverage with a fourteenth century tea spoon and offered me a lapis lazuli sugar bowl.

'North Coburg, Sir?' I smiled and concentrated on not spilling my drink. I love a good shot of coffee.

'Really?' he answered suddenly tired. 'Why?'

'It's cheap and multicultural,' I answered sipping the scrumptious stuff and listening to capes and mortarboards colliding in the hall. The entire English Faculty wore capes and mortarboards as though they taught at Cambridge University or something. But it was only Posh so I wondered why that was. I guess appearances count for much in this surface appearance world where I have preferred the look of a derelict, although I don't sleep in my rags.

He said 'sort of' a great deal, as it turned out.

'We've sort of read your comment articles in *The Age* over the millennia and sort of wondered whether you might enjoy the change of pace here at Posh where many students are ambitious to also appear in "Comment" because so many read it in Melbourne, even if they swear they don't. The Year Twelves in particular are desperate to be published in the daily press and several of them want to go on to book publishing that shall lead them to fame and more money than their divorced parents ever earned in their life times. Your job, should you accept our offer would be to mentor eight-foot-high spoilt boys who don't understand the value of a dollar and get them into print. Our contract is on my desk and I don't think our cheque shall bounce. You would live in and have two secretaries named Marie who shall prepare your evening bath with their own palms and cook stunning solo banquets for you to enjoy after getting the Year Elevenses literate. Care to take a peek. I'm stepping outside for a gasper.'

I enjoyed him walking up and back in the jade green and leafy miniature water-falled courtyard stuffed with gold fish and various dripping wet ferns. He smoked two Sullivan And Powell Oval Shaped Turkish Filters right down to their butts as he leisurely perved on the backside of the gardener whose sex couldn't be detected but looked nice. He stepped in again and I'd already signed and witnessed it myself. He gave it to me then I gave it to my interior breast pocket striving to keep remembering that it was there. I tend to forget things like important documents or even wives.

I was forgetting my marriage now after three terrible years of gnashing my dentures. I was so in love with her for so long then suddenly she meets someone upon the net and I went. But time sutures all wounds and the dreadful nicks and gashes in my aorta are over. The pain abates because you love all you see in the sewer that is life. You forget hate because it burdens you like a receipt from Office Works. You don't have the foggiest clue how to live but somehow there are others-than-you whom God likes. I was taken down from the long cross of unemployment and given Posh. He took me like a lamb to the great hall of privileges where masters took off their robes and looked like shit-kickers again; it is an amazing thing to witness that, the taking off of importance like a jumper. Hundreds of rich bastards hoeing into enormous pots of volcanic mashed pumpkin and a ton block of oily heart-attack Shepherd's Pie shoved roughly on that. They attacked their home-grown spinach with the same relish they correct a boy's grammar.

The Geography Ladies ate hardest and to my shock belched. The History Men sipped archaic soup from a tureen from Babylon. The Principal himself curtsied to me in a playful sort of way and beamed he did when he gave me my nosh with steam hammering out of every tentative fork-hole in it. It was more tucker than I'd get through in a decade. I wasn't in fact hungry as I'd had my oats in the morning as well as a half a Wagon Wheel on the train. My car was flat.

The Priest sat at the head of the enormous dining table and blessed us all for pigging in. He welcomed me as Barry McKenzie, confusing me with a Barry Humphries character, but I couldn't have cared less. The holy chap spoke of the need for mercifulness then they all ate their heads off in a large rush. I poked at my meal and just couldn't come at it no matter what. The Principal told me his mother had croaked it last night, but then he winked at me, so I wasn't sure what to feel from this odd but friendly and familiar gentleman. At one stage he punched his pumpkin.

I ended up swapping spots a few times because after the sweet of jellied pears they all were. I chatted eagerly with the librarian who told me she had been fucked by The Devil. I ended with more coffee then the Deputy Principal escorted me to a great room right up high called The Atrium which was the spot for my classes beginning Period 6: a Double Drama Lesson. It was quite warm so the overhead electric fans were switched on and that was much happier for me. In the end about forty gigantic things came in demanding publication and subsequent fame. They were rather aggressive in manner and throat acne not to mention yellow-heads on their chins and their eyes were full of hate. I got a trifle self-conscious in respect of their look. I had no supervision and they had guaranteed it. I was the only teacher in charge of forty thugs.

One great big rich freak was just staring at me doing saliva bubbles he then blew in the air cross-eyed. His body was so muscular and gross the elbow-sleeves eventually exploded whilst he sharpened his expensive pencil with a flick-knife. He belched too due to loads of Coke that he purchased from the canteen and threw down en-route to Drama With Dickins.

Another child had a head bigger than anyone's outside of Vaudeville or Barnum And Bailey. His head just went on and on upward to the ceiling till it stopped at his hair. He had a sort of retarded dandiness about him and had a pocket watch you'd expect on a man out of the Nineteenth Century and he seemed by his air to have the numbers to be the power of the group. Two smaller lads were meeker or at least meek. They could barely see over the top of my desk. A very tough boy called 'Thing' proceeded without any explanation to punch the door in. The blows that door stood were outstanding for if they'd connected with my jaw I'd have been dead a minute in. We watched him savage into the paintwork and handle of that door till it got very broken. He got very puffy and sweaty by the time the whole door came off and then he had its handle wrapped in his bloodied hand as he lay unconscious on the carpet with his tongue hanging out.

No one in our group cared.

One of the twins asked me how you begin writing, if that's not an awkward question, Sir? I said it's probably better to be original than clichéd. He looked temporarily crestfallen just as his fellow twin did.

'Can we write about incest?' he asked then added that he hoped that wasn't obvious. I didn't know how to answer that question so I didn't bother saying anything. 'Can we write about my mother's relationship with organised crime in Carlton, Sir?' Yes. 'Have you ever dined with The Carlton Mafia, Sir?' Yes, but I had to pay.

We wrote dialogue to do with drive-bys and that satisfied most of them for one period at least.

'Don't forget boys don't murder the narrator too early on because you sort of need him to complete the scene. Try to write with pleasure and boys – not too much rape.'

They got to and we shared and the librarian was happy about it and told me I had to know just about every thief in Melbourne, which I clearly do and am very proud about that fact. We had bagged about twenty minutes' worth of believable dialogue mostly due to the fact that a lot of the boy's dads drank with famed murderers, so the quotations came effortlessly.

I caught my train at South Yarra railway station with all the sweaty losers and in a way it was a relief to smell most of them again, my fellow pong! Hot night with hundreds of divorced chaps trying to remember bringing deodorant to the office, hundreds of lonely overweight hearts tapping away for the scarcity of Love. Breadcrumb men reading their own eulogies in the paper through two-dollar glasses. Others of them like me, teachers trying to lift the masses in the hopeless fight against dumbness. The on-going war with the mortgage you can't meet. The fight with groceries to the bitter Weet Bix end. Fathers got granted access to children who loathe them anyway because their weak dads have tried to buy love via overseas holidays to Disneyland the kids are bored with before they fly out. Mothers trying to bribe brat girls with expensive clothes that no one can afford. Sweaty workers staring at the Nylex Sign over Richmond wondering why it's there. Hairy bandy legs belonging to ugly pairs of off-shore shorts belonging to eunuchs of the disappearing hoi poloi.

I got out at Princes Bridge as I couldn't breathe on that train and swallowed half a dozen pain killers with a pot of fresh beer at Young And Jacksons Hotel in Flinders Street. Ten thousand other English teachers had the same idea, apparently, there were so many of them there, all proferring ten buck notes in eager swap for an icy pot that drove the worry out for a minute; no more was wanted, certainly never the guarantee of a dreamy hour off fretting about things.

I met a teacher who taught French somewhere or other at the crush of drunken educators and we chatted inanely enough till it was time for his tram. I sat tired at the glossy bar and remembered where I rented in North Coburg, which was all I was trying to recall at the time. I have been re-reading a publication of Vincent Van Gogh's amazingly tender letters and at the crowded bar some of his sentences started writing themselves out again for my eyes, almost like the punishment for boys who can't spell a single thing and their teachers force them to do it over and over, not that you ever learn a thing like that. Punishment isn't writing. Joy is.

When I alighted the stinking Moreland tram I realised I was drunken and fell right over. A Greek woman pinched my seat with her carrots so I had to stand all the way when she did that. By the time I got to Moreland Road I needed to do wee but that wasn't very possible.

My next day at Posh College was windy and hot and the sky was in a bad mood. It wanted to rain a lot but was in a temper, a terrible temper, maybe the weather was uneducated and remained sulky. It was so humid that mortarboards wouldn't come off English

Masters' craniums. I was introduced at Monday Morning Assembly as one of Australia's greatest writers which was news to me.

I'd been to the bank last Friday and read the sour news that I had thirty cents.

The principal had me confused with Barry Oakley and in his speech told all he had never laughed so much in all his days than when he read *The Great McCarthy*. He even had his own signed copy and read some of it out, to which no one smiled for a single second, then wiping the tears out of his pince-nez he uttered looking happy at me: 'Just how do you comedy-makers write like this? Do tell us all here at Posh!'

I wanted to explain he had the wrong author but the next thing was the lacrosse results followed by recent drownings on the Yarra during canoe racing, regrettably but very annual. I wrote poems then taught future accountants who had size 50 shoes. It was strange to conduct such vastly different kids from last week's lot at Blueberry. I read somewhere once that Charles Darwin once said the difference between people is the difference between species and that is exactly how I felt at Posh after teaching happy fairies at Blueberry where I'd never been happier or felt teaching really stands for encouragement and that listening to kids is the way for us to learn.

These boys at Posh had legs so big they burst their shorts, I wondered why they wore shorts but they did until they exploded with testosterone. Their cocks were like horses' ones I'd seen at Flemington Race Track in the mounting yard. They brayed rather than talked and their minds were okay but when two of these giants started brawling and dry-humping I had to say something, as I was in charge without anyone to give me an intro, so I said, which is perfectly stupid and not like my personality at all-seeing, 'Darren I wonder if you could stop braining Hugh with that length of airconditioning metal. I don't think it's appropriate Darren and in any case he's actually covered in his own gore.

Darren replied as follows and this is exactly what he said under the big and pummelling boy, 'How do you know he's not enjoying it?'

Good point I replied and chalked up some half rhymes on the dusty filthy blackboard which they ignored and just went on assaulting one another, but in a very real sense doing the pummelling out of indifference. Some of the Year Twelves were over nine foot high and were obviously training as hit men and would later train in other disciplines such as cooking at Florentinos.

The double English lesson lasted a lifetime or 100 minutes; take your pick. One of them had read a bit of John Donne but got the title of his poem wrong and said to us, 'I really liked the John Donne one called "To His Mistress After I Fucked Her". I pointed out that it wasn't called that and he sat down losing all interest. '"To His Mistress Undressing" is the true title of your poem,' I pointed out, but he gave me the finger and left the room very put out. 'Same Fucking thing!,' said he as he swept into the corridor.

The kids roared with ape approval and swung along

the corridor after their spokes-ape. I didn't know what to do so I went to the staff lounge and helped myself to impressive percolated coffee that is grown in a rainforest by paid blacks it said on the can. The principal who thought I was Barry Oakley came along and read a tract of one of his favourite Oakley books to me then asked me to sign the preface, which I did as Barry Oakley.

To my considerable regret Posh College offered me permanency and I guess due to tough economic times, that are unvarying as the pox I reluctantly accepted the position as Head Of English. My duties were considerable and included free use of a permanent mortarboard whose silky tassle turned me on as it tickled my nose if I didn't watch it. I also got kitted-up in a Zorro cape that looked, I thought, wonderful on my working-class shoulders.

I gargled with a minty throat rinse the very second of awakening. I combed my fair hair in the shower to try to lend it an air of scrubbed authority, not that I'd ever had any. My entire existence has been nothing. Nothing on toast and no sex unless it was with a nightmare.

I had virtually consigned myself to continuous poorness and that drags on your soul and spirit after a heck of a lot of knocks, so the new teaching position came right on cue you'd be gratified to say to yourself. I started enjoying ruling-class breakfast that included stone-ground toast with a generous film of nude avocado on.

I read the press on my wonky breakfast table and wore a suitable suit, which I ironed using pornography. I exercised on my exercise bike that had a speedometer on it set on 100 kph. I motored out to Posh with all the other snobby English teachers of Melbourne which makes up half our population, I guess. I switched on ABC FM and enjoyed classical trombones on tramlines. In short I enjoyed myself and taught my mind that it's more enjoyable to be a privileged prick than an unemployable poet.

Whenever I parked in my permanent full-time staff parking space I felt a sexual charge previously unknown to me. I swore beneath my breath, my so-minty breath as I alighted my car if I spotted dog excreta either on my shoe or somehow coagulant on my treasured black taffeta mortarboard.

I made certain I never under any circumstances fumbled my reports or graded essays in the puddles of the sacred staff car park.

I always write my morning thoughts on vast amounts of endless Manila folders some lower-order Posh staff person gave me to scribble considerations upon. These fresh thoughts in my experience can prove invaluable if they're any good. They are usually not if the recipient of the folders is tucking into All Bran on skim milk. Precursor to understandable suicide.

I have to say I was completely corrupted from day one and began to talk like a snob to fellow English masters with their pseudo T.S. Eliot voices just about perfected on the toilet.

I adored the leisurely stroll down the corridors of advanced grammar and loved to step in a slightly bored way into a noun class or an adverb group of stuttering

Year Twelve youths perfecting their wits in a red-faced sort of way usually, with their stuttering masters in front of them leisurely rattling off *The Iliad* in Latin or even Australian. Heaven Forbid!

My work was to look dreadfully important all the time and being the ultimate imitator of life it was just so fun to do. I swished importantly up and down the highly-glossed parquetry and nodded to introspective Swiss librarians and winked at jaundiced Geography staff in such a winning way that was almost wicked but I wanted them to rest assured I would always remember countries they'd somehow forgotten, such as Keon Park let us say.

There was nothing in fact to do but sigh occasionally and nibble a digestive biscuit. The English Faculty were intimidated by me which is exactly what Posh wanted and I was perceptive at the sudden shifts of allegiance because that is what blind power means. All you need to do is be a mean bastard.

I liked the sound of my own cultivated voice and obviously so did the lesser ones there at Posh who almost soiled themselves when I wheeled round the corners with my mortarboard glaring at them and my dreadfully expensive Broughams creaking in tandem and the frightening and soul-quivering-sight of my cape flapping at them.

My twin secretaries got all excited when I came by and flurried about with things being Zerox'd at high-speed just to appear flat-out. I calmed them from time to time by just talking nicely.

I liked the boys in Year Twelve very much and although they were splendid chappies most of them were actually difficult to view as they were ten foot tall with thousands of yellow-heads. They positively burst through their grey cotton shorts with athletic calves the size of houses. Their idiotic mothers made them wear these preposterous shorts for some reason and the lads just put up with looking ridiculous in them, which displayed great manliness particularly if they were experiencing an unexpected hard-on.

They all wore hard-ons all the time and especially doing woodwork or metal work with their teachers actually having the same sorts of erections. Science can't ever explain this mystery satisfactorily.

Whenever it was woodcarving out came the hard-ons and the lads to their eternal credit just got on with them. I loved to view the lacrosse and observe my boys catching the flu out on the fields of praise as the other masters termed paddocks of special grasses.

The principal commissioned me one day to give a speech in the Great Hall on Leadership, he actually put a large cheque in my pigeon-hole for writing this and it didn't bounce, either, when I went to the bank in Glenferrie Road Hawthorn during my luncheon-break. I enjoyed writing the uplifting speech and read it out in my new Posh voice that styles itself on Winston Churchill. I even wore a monocle on stage and no boy laughed at me. I had the moment as they say in The Theatre.

I spoke grimly but most assuredly of the need for

control, not just in finance but the bedroom, of the need for reading if one is to be a real man. I recommended the critical study of Sigmund Freud, particularly if they wanted to run a pet shop after they graduated or even failed VCE. I told them not to get hooked on Channel Ten news on television because they exaggerate the truth at five at night and invariably frighten their steadfast viewers with terrifying visions of country bush fires only to follow that squeamish sequence with hot underwear ads.

I told them to keep a daily diary and record their every thought for nostalgic reading when they turned senile a few years later; they must have liked that remark as they whistled a lot and cheered me. I got a trifle close to the stand-up-microphone at one stage and my big red nose bumped into the sponge-thing at the top of its steel stem and I distorted something I'd written but no one appeared to notice this slight mishap.

I had a beautiful voice on me and milked the entranced applause the whole college afforded me. I was so sure I had a novel way with the truth and ended my speech by telling them to wear a condom. There was a slap-up luncheon after that and I was given shucked oysters marginally more real than those transmitted on cooking programs on Channel Ten each minute to sadden the poor. I was given Posh Broth a favourite of the gods and sipped it eagerly through a straw I found in my bag that morning.

After school Miss Winsome demanded to take me

home to her mansion in Hampton East where she introduced me to her husband who meditated in front of me on a flat cushion he'd bought off his fakir.

She had a groovy fit body on her but dyed black hair with a much-rinsed countenance that made her good-looking but plain except for her brilliant Hampton accent which is just like Queen Elizabeth's. She's taught at Posh for ages but was sick of being right. She told me in her parlour where her vile hubby couldn't hear us she intended an affair with me just as soon as all this educational nonsense left her free to do so. She came right over and caressed me and hugged her elegant body to my fucked one. Now I hadn't been hugged for years since my first wife decided to jettison me. The hug went on for ten minutes at least while her hubby meditated in the sitting room and as I listened carefully to her breasts and so-on it occurred to me it was a bit bloody dangerous to be going the grope with a married lady in her own six bedroom villa but possibly it was just terror.

He kept on meditating as she ran her lips across my ears and I wondered if she had any undies on. Then I tried to move my lonely god-damned chapped lips to converge on hers but she instinctively pulled away but refused not to touch me.

As she caressed my lonesome hair I tried to remember if she taught Latin or English but just drew a long blank. She sure was a pretty lady but I didn't know if she was serious about me or not. Her son came in and she just about screamed, 'What the fuck do you want?' she said in Latin to him. I recognised the saying immediately.

He looked crestfallen slightly and sat down like a girl. He was really skinny and looked terribly interesting which is pretty crucial in Year Ten. He wore long black frizzy hair and long limbs like lost pieces of a Meccano Set Puzzle.

We all sat and he read us pretentious recent prose from his latest novel his meditating father intended to publish at Office Works.

Strive as I might I just didn't get it. It seemed to be written in love of Fielding. Or it could've been a cricket book. I wanted to make love to his sexy mother right there and then for she showed zero interest in the unasked for reading by her praying-mantis son and continues to stare at me like a love-struck hen.

She accompanied me to the car and kissed me passionately on my arm that clutched my steering wheel, a thing in my imaginary love life that had never occurred before. I'd never been kissed on my steering wheel before, then she drifted inside to watch the television with her hypersensitive family of pseudo-Indians who all are obsessed with fakirs and Calcutta because they're always flying there first class.

I got home and found many domestic accounts rammed hard in my letterbox and that as per usual snails had perforated all my mail but declined to digest my gas and light bill. I sighed and took my mortarboard and cape off and stuffed round looking for the key to the front that was in my hand. I tidied up the slum by leaving it. I went up the Arab's in Sickening Road and had just enough cash for a plate of dreadful boiled chook that had a nose still in it.

That cook must have got behind in his work and got too close to his own fowls. But it wasn't too inedible after all and I washed it back with several cigarettes. Who am I? Where was I? I'm a teacher of ups and also downs who works in hundreds of sorts of schools, obviously now. I didn't miss my wife but I was lost and feeling awful in the hot chookery. They just wanted to hose out the fat and do the register as it was obviously getting on a bit. But somehow I felt at home there in the grot.

I got home and played all the messages. One was from me. I was practising the recording bit of it so I was on first so I tried to patiently erase me. I got rid of me and listened to the next which was the lady I'd just been hugging in East Hampton. She said she was thinking of me even whilst shagging her hubby. I didn't really wish to preserve that one and I certainly didn't need my son to overhear it. He never misses a single trick and I didn't want any embarrassment for him or for me, but of course with me I am nothing but an embarrassment. That goes without saying.

I took off my jumper and changed my legs into new jocks I buy at Barkly Square in packs of offshore six and thought the red pair suited my sex organ. I ironed my cape and mortarboard with its important silk tassel and left both to dry on the tea table in readiness for tomorrow. What is tomorrow? Is it in any sense like today? I entered my bedroom like the final guest of The Black Hole Of Calcutta.

The Paucity of Dreams

I tried very hard to have hot dreams about her the sexy Latin mistress but she didn't come. What came was insomnia and hotness even with two fans on my bum. The overhead fan twirled in its melancholic manner but it didn't soothe my savage dentures.

I just lay there feeling like a charlatan or possibly a cheetah or a fakir of Coburg-North. How do you rent a slum in Coburg and run the English Faculty at Posh College? The truth I know will out and I would be outed by some arsehole teacher who was jealous I was porking the Latin teacher there, not that I was but I certainly wanted to. I got up and fried black pud in the miserable opshop fry pan but was out of margarine so I poured in a very tired way heaps of cheap imported vegetable oil all over myself until I was satisfied. I sat at my tea table and wished I was dead but ate the pud.

As my false teeth ground the muck into my worthless oesophagus I hated myself but was still hungry so I cleaned it up and then cast the dish into the clogged sink. How long would I toil at Posh until they or I myself tumbled me as a true English fakir? I didn't get a wink and had difficulty driving up the Eastern Freeway in morning peak, partly because it wasn't the right way to go to Posh in the first instance. I corrected my mindset and got into Toorak Road and then onto Posh which is a few miles on in dense BMW traffic: four trillion glossy black BMW's driven by cooking teachers.

I trod on my mortarboard and my cape fell off me as I went in but my secretaries bent to pick them up and I promised them a pay rise.

I examined my daybook and swiftly saw I had a meeting with parents at 10 o'clock in Interview Room 2, which happened to be in some place I didn't know. I sipped Rat Sack as the concerned parents came in, well not so much rat poison but Early Grey. They looked anxious about their son's futures as if they possibly didn't have any. 'My son hates me,' explained a father and I passed him a tissue. 'My son casts ice cream wrappers all over our home,' sobbed the second. 'My son votes for Labor every single time there's a vote,' cried number three daddy. The more they pointed out what cunts their sons were the more I agreed with them. 'What can I do with my son if he hangs our dog as he has sworn he shall do?' cried the first. I said it was a poor idea to let a son hang his pet and let it go at that. Just so long as you yourself don't execute it, I pointed out and that remark as not only Head Of English at Posh but as a perfect Christian. But nothing relieved them. Not a sausage.

I got the concerned parents to sit ever closer to their sage, me. I used my old familiar mellow English voice on them that included loads of 'It seems to me' and 'not quite the done thing, really' and 'rather!' and I got through to them in one go. I asked them whether their children enjoyed literature after dinner but they didn't. They neither read nor laughed and were lonely some place in between that of course would shortly be unemployment. The fathers were all members of the Brighton Yachting Club and looked it. They puffed pipes and wore blazers which is all you have to do to gain selection. The mothers were all fund-raisers for ill-nourished blacks in South Africa and had baggy eyes and backsides like bookshelves.

One mother came onto me in the car park and asked me for sex. I didn't know her that well and couldn't recall her first or second name; not really. I said she wasn't my type although I had no clue as to what my type really was. We shook hands and left it at that. But whilst at my desk a little later she telephoned me and asked me why I didn't return all her mobile telephone calls from last year. I said I'd only just met her and she hanged up or is that hung up.

I found I must tell you the parent-teacher interviews trying at our son's high school, maybe it was because I was working so hard at Posh as well as not communicating that well with my ex. One particular meeting I found emotionally wracking happened at about six in the evening at his ugly school which is a giddy labyrinth of a hovel and it's very hard to understand its winding staircases or how to get anywhere when you hate the place anyway. I didn't know where to meet my ex and son and just wandered round like an Arab.

After ages I stumbled onto them and we sat rather sheepishly and waited for his teacher to come, but they never do, or at least they come when you least expect their outline in gloomy halls. She turned up looking both young and masterful, very modern which is to say severe, all in black like a walking BMW. She didn't ask who were were and that suited as we didn't, or at least I didn't, know who we were, I never will.

Our son seemed calm and collected enough and gave a powerpoint display about racism that I nodded to but couldn't follow. The teachers said he was going very well at school and that was it. I was handed a folder full of photocopied reports from some software somewhere but the only thing I could understand was his beautiful smile on top of the main a4 page that had a big metal staple through it. I thought that was barbaric.

We didn't exchange a word on the dark and winding way out of his school. I found my car and congratulated our son on his overhead projection or whatever it is they are called and he said so sincerely, 'Thanks Dad!'

I drove home like a dead guy up desolated Moreland Road where they were constructing either a gibbet or block of flats; it was impossible to see a difference architecturally or spiritually. I got in and read all my threats out of the letterbox and swore once or twice as my opshop readers broke because they are cheap trash and then I really couldn't concentrate on my domestic accounts as everything was a blur.

The education of the human soul doesn't respond to commerce or collusion. No matter how many times my ex told me I looked well I felt terrible and found living alone worse than imaginable and especially the hopping into bed alone the most devastating experience after decades of marriage.

I tried to locate happy thoughts but the future looked like Posh College with no one in the building except a hanged janitor.

I tossed like a salad until five in the morning and very nearly didn't go in today. But after a hot bath and writing out cheques for my gas and power and rental I felt much better indeed. I didn't have any breakfast and desperately needed to do a shop at the supermarket but just hadn't got around to it.

I balanced my mortarboard on better and enjoyed putting my front indicator on and swept into the fabulous Posh Permanent Staff Car Park. I spoke eloquently at our morning briefing but somehow confused Posh College with the Western Front and began to speak of the horrors of war instead of curriculums. I even quoted from Siegfried Sassoon but really they didn't mind even though they'd never heard of him before.

In the afternoon I sat weeping hard as hard in my desk because of the parent-teacher-interviews of the evening before where I had felt so devastated listening to our son speak well but to divorced parents, not that he seems to mind but it impacted on me terribly and the weight of that impenetrable isolation came up on me from behind my spirit and it got me in its sure grip. Half the country's parents are divorced. The other half are deceased.

The two secretaries poured their master several stiff black coffees and I sipped a biscuit or three until I felt better; but it took half a packet of Monte Carlos to do that. I went off and had a word in the headmaster's ear-hole and explained I was feeling a tad down and he showed pity about that to my amazement and took me to Brighton Pier for the day. We had a refreshing stroll along the ancient and dilapidated pier and watched the weather change from calm to choppy. We threw our expensive mortarboards into the bracing sou' wester.

He wasn't a bad egg at all and spoke of enjoying his freedom after toiling away for centuries at Posh and only finding real joy in walking the Brighton Pier and throwing stout bottles at fish. We darned-well took our socks off and wriggled our nude feet on a friendly bench. Some uneducated fisherfolk threaded their hooks with dim sums or spring rolls and did well to catch many fish as the head and I looked on.

It was really swirly as anything and we just perched exactly where we were and pontificated on education as a complete and utter waste of time and money, apart from the secretaries and nice desks. He admitted his wife was lonely and had had a bad breakdown and that of a night he read Brer Rabbit to her which she liked; however she didn't like Brer Bear much. He had no fun with her and used to leave her at obscure country railway stations but somehow she invariably found her way home. She whined and wept all the time, he explained to me and he was forced to put her on a leash and walk her round the block to calm her body.

We recited from the great poets and repaired to his home where his demented wife howled in a hedge; he put on classical music which we both delighted in and then he passed me a large scotch and I slaked it in the one grateful gulp. He told me he had a rabbit hutch but that was in another country and I replied that I understood where he was coming from, but really I just couldn't.

We ended up dead drunk with whisky bottles like a raft all over the room. He insisted on driving me home to North Coburg but it was pretty bloody dangerous in the extreme and he kept asking me all the way what I did for a living. We picked up a blind hitchhiker

I made a late-night snack for the principal and blind hitchhiker of toasted cheese and tomatoes on toast and they greedily wolfed them back not noticing the blue mould triangles of filth I'd gouged out of my stale Vietnamese bread I get for ninety cents a ton in Sickening Road.

'Tremendous; tremendous old crust!' they chorus'd as one. We watched a bit of telly but the hitchhiker couldn't make head or tail of the show and stormed away in a profound stink. The headmaster and myself played poker till late then he crashed on my good sofa without his mortarboard on. I put my cape over him and he slept remarkably soundly till six when eventually we enjoyed our cereal together. Corn Flakes on Gin.

I worked very hard for Posh College but was pleased when my tenure come to its end after two good years of elitism. I'm a very capable leader of course but probably it's much better if I stick to working-class schools. I taught at Aniseed North next. The high school.

Aniseed North South High

In the end the longed-for-offer arrived in my letter box from the not anticipated Aniseed North South West High School, where I'd never taught before but would willingly give it a crack. I pride myself on being able to teach in any school because it's always been in the Antipodean spirit to improvise no matter how tough the unexpected conditions may be. I telephoned Miss Gnarled at this new bush place, although to be strict it was over 1250 years old, possibly only 125, and she seemed to have her noggin on properly, for she said to me, 'It shall be absolutely marvellous to have a writer like Barry Breen as our guest prose author, because we here at work have long marvelled at his style which is nothing short of genius, don't interrupt, and so we shall meet you Mr Breen where the bus pulls in, having de-camped from Southern Cross Station and come to us via Ballarat. You shall stay with us at no charge rather than put us to the inconvenience of some pretentious motel. You shall teach in a three-piece suit and remain sober throughout your paid tenure. It is pretty cold here at the minute so bring a hat and a pencil box for when we shove you in with the Preps.'

Then she was gone so I ironed my old suit and vest and was startled to see I could at a pinch (or several of them) still squeeze into my pants that looked not too bad apart from boasting frayed cuffs and the bottom a bit shiny if you looked with scrutiny. I found my hat and then put it on. I then ironed my leather wallet and was glad to see it still undid and zipped-up and had lots of groovy sections for inserting my railway tickets, change for the daily newspapers and that it fitted in my back pocket no problem.

I put the old milk in the fridge and put the margarine lid on with sure savagery as 'waste not want not' had to be my cut-price maxim. I got the Sickening Road tram to Southern Cross although inexplicably the suffocating tram stopped at Moreland Road where it farted hard then chugged to a complete halt. The driver made some incoherent speech about roadwork and we got thrown off.

The bus went to the city via every bump in Melbourne and took an extra half an hour so I reverberated off like a squash ball having struck a brick wall. I was in Collins Street, a bit frightened I have to say of missing my connection, but there was nothing coming and nothing I could ever do about that.

I met the most refreshing boy I'd ever bumped into there and he was over-excited about the prospect of climbing Cradle Mountain in Tasmania and getting liberated from his family and looking forward to sleeping in caves and going canoeing on rapid white water or whatever it is. After twenty minutes' worth of amiable conversation I honestly felt closer to him than my own ex. The tram down Collins Street was packed with backpackers but he was the only one I could relate to or wanted to. He was like an earlier model of me before introspection and education stepped in the way of joy. He was just so joyous!

I felt a real tug when he got off and wished he was

my friend a bit longer; already I was sensing my old nemesis clinical depression sneaking up on me, but as always I misdiagnosed myself. It was just divorce. I bought my ticket surprising myself with self-knowledge for I pulled out my mint-new Seniors Card with my Savings Card and was rapt to see it got me nearly 50% off. The Indian ticket guy threw my change at me and I went and did wee.

In the public loo of the vast station two ticket collectors could plainly be seen up each other but I paid no heed to them blokes. I had better things to look at such as gumtrees and blowflies and to get out my diary and enter my sacred observations, a thing I always do on country train rides to idle away the insane boredom.

I got out my completely new NAB biro and wrote a perfect prose account of the look of the train that included a deceased crow that had got itself electrocuted, happily.

I wrote what I saw. Silly old ladies chatting aimlessly about mucus in kitten's eyeballs or whatever inane topic belted through their brain-damage. Nice old men talking about catching a fox 100 years ago just out of Bendigo. The old bloke next to me started to ear-bash me something stupid about his 60 years in the wire industry. He had actually ear-bashed me earlier on the platform about wire-manufacture as he witnessed it.

I had found it dreary then when we met on the seat in front of the Aniseed train but had the bad luck to sit next to him again and he immediately got into me again in an accusatory way to be certain. He also raved about his lifetime Australia Wide train ticket that permitted him to go anywhere on the house, even Aniseed.

'Do you believe in Australian wire,' he demanded of me and I tried to look away but he bloodshot eye was elliptical. He glared at me with menacing foul-smelling rotten teeth and punched my innocent arm hard; it really hurt and for an instant it occurred to me to deck him, but he had to be 100 if he were a day, so I pulled back my furious fist.

With his heinous head a fraction from me he shoved an album of wire portraiture at me, this big bulgy album crammed to the hilt with photos of wire factory Christmas parties and the like. He punched each wire photo as he italicised his recollections by hissing the facts of them in my ear. 'Like I said to yer earlier yer not interested in our nation's wire are yer?'

I gave him the biggest glare of my life which he ignored and so I went to the canteen and politely ordered a pot of tea and toast and we pulled up somewhere way out west and the country train hissed to a stop and I saw all these squinty-eyed cute little bunnies. The paddocks were crammed with rabbits but no other thing whatever, and then I spied the wire raconteur out in the paddocks just staring back at the train. Clearly he needed soon to be shot.

The railway authorities ran out and gave him his medication and carted him screaming like a demon back to his seat; they told him off in no uncertain terms for running away like that and one of the guards said a bear might have eaten him, then the wire man wept into his large and ornamental wire-making palms; some bitter tears of his twin waterfalls splashing on my home-made tomato and cheese sandwiches and that really put me off him.

He was heavily sedated just before Ballarat and had to be stretchered off at Aniseed-proper, with many people very concerned about his welfare.

I got off and met my host and was whisked away to her expensive country home in the watercolour set hills just out of Aniseed. Her grouchy husband asked me how long was I staying but for some reason I replied I didn't smoke; I guess my mind was tired-out. He threw my bag on the spare-room bed and went and had a big feed.

His wife had a big feed with him but I was uninvited so I suppose I felt a bit miffed about that and just sort of sat in my room until they were through. I could hear their sticky big custard plates landing in the hot water of the sink and them drinking out there. I went in about ten and the host asked me what was up. I said that I was a bit hungry, in fact famished and she looked a bit put-out and sighed massively at her pig of a husband who sighed just as massively back. I sighed too.

'Jesus I don't really want a coffee but I'd better have one otherwise the police will book me on the way to get him a fucking burger!' screamed my principal-host and her guy swore at me and downed his claret and reversed their tractor out of the haybarn. That was an inspired choice of vehicle for it must have taken two hours to get to the Aniseed main drag and find a hamburger shop still trading. She said she'd wait but she didn't and drove the unroadworthy conveyance back to the farm in order to get drunk good and proper. I ordered one with the lot and the in-bred girl told me she was just a work-experience lady and the burger was rotten in the end and all burnt and took an hour.

I paid and wanted to get at it indoors but she said it was too late to be neat and locked the burger shop double-doors, so I had to eat it with blunt knife and fork out on the veranda with yodelling lorrikeets staring at every dropped crumb.

I had to walk back to the host's farm so it was quite late when I got into bed, maybe even six in the morning so I didn't get much shut-eye before she kicked the door in to rouse me from my slumbers. She looked pretty good for an alcoholic school principal and even her idiotic husband looked partly sober as he helped himself and herself to endless stiff black percolated coffees. I had to reach over them to get at a cup.

I was introduced to the Grade 7s as a 'city writer with a wealth of experience getting E.C.T'. I taught well and enjoyed the pupil's exuberant company and they wrote with style and liked my praise of Dylan Thomas who they assumed was from Mortlake. She didn't wait for me after work so I had to walk back to the farm again with no hope of any kind getting a lift from anything but a dead ox.

They were hard at the bottle again as soon as I got in so I ignored them both and read from both Proust and *The Aniseed Street Directory* until they fell over utterly spent from cooking sherry on the filthy linoleum floor with her parent-teacher reports all mucked up from both squashed cigarette butts and cheap wine. I ate my chop and vegetables with them unconscious on the floor and boiled their kettle and composed tea for my enjoyment. I dragged them both by their boot heels into their bed and with Herculean effort shoved them on the mattress where hopefully the bush buzzards could have them.

In the morning they were not merely still breathing but showered and both shaved and tucking into vast amounts of bubble'n'squeak on hot thick and yummy toast fresh from their own mill. As she erratically drove me into work on the third day of my week stay she deliberately ran over a child near a bridge across a skinny creek. 'That's one less we don't have to try and educate!' she shrieked and tooted the horn hard, in fact it gave me a headache as soon as she blasted it. It was a ute she drove as they had sheep that needed to get dagged or hung.

I had the Grade Ones first up and was feeling a bit queasy about the head-count but she explained to the kids that life was cruel and left it to me to get on with it. Some of the poor confused little buggers wept like anything because they suspected she'd done it but they couldn't prove it so they tried to concentrate on their lesson with me. We did cartoons of bush graves, mostly.

In the afternoon the cops came and she was charged with one case of first-degree murder, handcuffed and escorted to jail in Aniseed. Her husband was charged with being an accessory after the fact, even though he wasn't in the utility at the time of the crime. There was a kind of post-mortem after school and many bereaved parents brought personal items to form a shrine to the dead lad run over by his own school principal. Thongs and a compass.

The husband drank even harder that night after I walked home yet again and he swallowed disinfectant with the wine he was that out of it. 'It'll be in all the fucking papers!' he screamed until I quit the kitchen. I could hear him having a fit from my room so I went for a long and solitary stroll right round the hills of dear Aniseed.

I saw such strange things in the scrub such as a fox with a condom on. A horse made out of barbed wire with a burning Ku Klux Klan cross in it. A murdered Geography teacher. A nail bag and a hammer with moss on it. A lost map of how to get to Melbourne and a huge unmarked mass grave of teachers buried forever.

I went back and he was asleep with their mangy dog in their shared kennel. In the morning he was scrubbed, showered and shaved with no sign of drink on him and he passed me a box of Cheerios and he personally sliced my big banana for me and added farm-fresh milk on my proffered bowl and he filled it up cheerier than the product. 'I've just seen the light, brother!,' he barked and gave me a tender reading from the Holy Bible and after re-reading Genesis on the bumpy track to school he apologised for his unfriendliness as well as his murdress wife's unfriendliness over the past week.

'She's just a bitch that's all, not that I'm any better, but just because she killed a kid doesn't excuse her lack of table etiquette and all that basic rudeness of hers. She may hang you know and that will really be a black mark against her.'

He met me after school on day four and he escorted me through the murderous walls of Aniseed Insanity Jail where I could hear the moaning of whipped girls and hoarse lamentations of hanged kids. The atmosphere was worse than the House of Representatives.

He gave me a friendly little hit of the tennis ball on the public courts in the front of the long-shut mad house and I could easily detect wails of people in Hell in some way or other right in front of me. I could see their faces in the most woeful way; they all looked like Met Card Ticket examiners.

He drove me all around Aniseed to see the shops like the fish and chip one but it had been long deserted due to lack of interest. There was a cinema albeit on fire. I loved Aniseed after that and even now can see people getting cut down out of plane trees.

On the Friday I got a lift to the station and read all about my host running over the son of the mayor near a bridge and the fact that she never stopped so it was not just a hit and run but murder in the first degree. On page two there was a topless horse. I got back home at least with income as the school had paid me Casual Relieving Teacher rates for five days so I had the rent covered, just.

A Bit of a Fright in the Street

Having got home my recollections of all that had gone before vanished and I went into my automaton imitation perfectly, knowing all the moves by heart as they are tutored by the greatest teacher who ever lived: loneliness. I sat terribly uncomfortably upon my much-kicked bottom on my rental vinyl lounge room carpet and simultaneously sipped restorative tea and viewed Channel Ten *Eye Witness News* and that always terribly relaxes me after a long day at the school. They're all long, the days are.

To my aghast brain the pictures flitted straight away without pause of absolute barbarity being perpetrated in the City Square of Melbourne. The cameras went in tight indeed to capture heart-stopping footage of riot cops kicking and then beating children who were protesting about Global Greed in a peaceful and bearded way, in fact the look of those puritan and protesting kids put me in mind of the hippies doing sit-ins, passively having a go at the ruling-classes 40 years ago.

I was shocked and spilt my arty ti-tree tea that I bought at a pretentious oil and perfume bar in Carlton called Husk. When I'd gone into that precious boutique shop and requested politely the rare ti-tree tea the erotic girl tending shop fell about in mirth that a man looking like a cave dweller such as myself could ask for something like that. 'Aren't you the truck guy parked out the back?' she snorted out loud in perfect incredulity of me wanting a new beverage.

As I paid for the tea I noticed a woman fork over a fortune for an American book entitled *To Smell Your Body Is Love At Its Most Profound*, written by some prosperous guru of imported lotions such as buttock dew.

As I tuned in with my weepy eyes my mucus mind beheld such alarming pictures they'd wake the dead no problem. Enormous brainwashed police ladies repeat-kicking children's craniums right in and then hurling them into great white steel division vans. The sound was recorded too of fists entering young jaw cavities and rods being belted over kid's faces. The sequence went on for over ten minutes and I found myself calling out, with no one there to hear me

'No! Stop it! That's enough cop violence!'

Not long after I ran the boring bath and got in to contemplate what I'd just seen, and in my fevered imagination the blood covered batons rained right down on my gored knees that were being bitten by wolverines right in my own tub, my own rental property. I went to bed early and fell asleep upon the instant, making a last minute mental note to shout myself a reasonably new pillow as the two I sleep on resembled rejected donor livers.

Mull

Last night I ran out of gas in the city somehow and pulled the pump out of the pump-thing and began swearing to myself because nothing came out. Then I jumped in the air somewhat because an amplified voice screamed 'PUMP SEVEN REPORT TO FRONT OFFICE'. You have to pay the amount of gas to the jerk in his mummified office before he'll switch it on for you. I really resented that idea and nearly yelled at him but what would be the point as well as the fact he had a snarling wolf by the cash register who was salivating at me. I didn't need to be eaten by a wolverine.

One nice school I taught poetry at was Mull Primary but on the first day there the bosses had invited lots of other Grade Twos over so I had to draw big cartoons sort of twelve-foot square with a decent Jumbo Texta and 800 kids aged about ten in all kinds of shapes and conditions followed my step-by-step as well as a lot of fat and skinny teachers doing the cartoon too.

There was a lot of yelling and squabbling as the sheets of paper were thrown at them like a chicken farmer casting wheat to hungry fowls kind of thing; it was annoying because I just hate wasting perfectly good paper like that. One child had the eye on him cut with the pinpoint edge of a flying square of cartridge paper and the eye bled profusely so the deputy principal had to whiz her off to Casualty because there were too many crook kids in the cramped sick bay.

I got through the first raucous lesson okay and the Jumbo Black Texta didn't go all dry. I hate it when I have to draw for kids and the bored teachers hand you a had-it Texta. At Morning Tea all I saw were millions of male silver Velcro-attired long distance cyclists all leaning on their phallus saddles sipping tea looking like Tony Abbott who is at the moment of writing the Leader of the Opposition.

In the end or the beginning which is the finish with a bit more lustre on it, it dawned on me that to teach at any institution at all was better somehow than being six feet under. I went for a residency at a women's jail when I was young with a black beard rather than snow-white-pubes. I got it to my surprise, this was in West Australia and was billeted with screws (as the female officers were crudely termed) and the contract promised me a good wage with paid holiday leave as well as super: a thing I'd never known before at any other school. But this was jail and I was all theirs.

It was a trifle trying having to rinse supper plates with huge black ladies who'd quit drink. They furiously chainsmoked however and I was forever scooping up their cascading hot ashes. There were just six of them in this in-bred hostel type arrangement and it was pretty clean on the Monday morning but you should've seen it after the Tuesday. Filth and nothing but.

The black lady screws were difficult to take, what with their neurotic way of handling withdrawal of booze which was to be in denial continually and just shake their heads and say they were clean but their savage mood-swings made it only too obvious they were hanging out and badly. The hospitality lacked kindness and that is the one essential ingredient you rather need when you board. The native ladies in solitary I taught by listening and that worked since I didn't upset their sensitivities by fetching in notepads or clutching slippery pens or pencils or set up any tape recorders.

It was upsetting to listen carefully to lady axe murderers who seemed unruffled entirely by putting a Canadian root splitter through the diseased brain of their errant husband. The first woman I met in fact had done her family and then successfully put in for a Three-Year Literature Board Fellowship fully supported by the sons and daughters who survived; this is presumably half sisters, half brothers who had just heard about the slaughter from afar but who had always suspected the lady had a nice prose style.

This wonderful murderess sat with her sinning black face all concealed by her big hands with the pink on the backs of them. She was all in shadow, the way the cell was lit and she fluttered and jumped a bit when I looked at her most unjudgingly. She was fat and hideous and had awful scabs and sores all over her big body. She spoke fluently about being beaten until she could not bear it one more blow and remarked on how her Daddy raped her when she was two and her brothers did as well in their awful shanty out in the Nulla.

'I just couldn't hack what they thought of me and did to me so I done the lot,' she hoarsely whispered and asked me for a Winfield Blue that I gave and she did it to the filter in one drag. 'They gave me life which is more than my own family gave me, which was death,' she laughed out loud. After listening with due care for two hours she began to write things down that were all to do with growing up in Hell apart from her rapture of colouring pencils from the mission and her joy at drawing trees and mountains in her dilapidated drawing book, which she still drew in in her cell.

We wrote a stream of consciousness poem, a long one, together charting her recollections and admissions of failure, such as murdering her loved ones or hated ones is better probably. I wasn't trying to be her companion or friend even temporarily but someone had to help the poor thing to cheer up and that fell to me as the resident author in jail.

I wrote a play with the ladies and the jail put on a rehearsed reading only none of the ladies could read, well not that well, but after a few stumbles we managed to produce it to an appreciative gathering, mostly of parole officers.

I found it hard on the Sunday which was the birthday of one of the guards and so they did a big barbecue and handed out boxes of grog and two screws rolled joints of very strong dope and they even hired an ambulance at tremendous expensive to be on stand-by just in case.

In the end this black lady and I went down the creek and had erotic sex completely stoned and wasted on cheap wine. Her body was the first black skin I'd ever been encouraged to touch and she was a strong and committed lover indeed who never tired of turning me on. She recited *Clancy Of The Overflow* to me, which seemed an odd choice for a black beauty like her but what the heck.

The next week back at work she wouldn't look at me and cut me out. It was just like fucking with white ladies, just as negative. But I got on with my job and concentrated on listening and digging the wax from both ears, sitting in their claustrophobic cells with them unjudgingly. It is a funny thing but in a racist land like Australia it seems always so perfectly natural to be the friends of Aboriginals. It is so hard to meet one in any situation, especially when like me you are a teacher in a school. I've never met a Koori school principal, not once during four long decades.

Some of the tales told to me just about made me completely keel over they were beyond sad and beyond sanity. Even though Kevin Rudd said sorry from his idiot card on television the harm done to them is irreparable. I felt a compelling peace working with Kooris and loved them in a new way and was grateful to their leaders for giving me the teaching work.

One day I won't forget was my last one and I had a double English with black guys who were stoned on something, in fact one guy was brazenly toking away on a joint the size of his didj. He was stroking the magnificent bosoms of an erotic black girl and blowing dope with her hand down his strides in the front row of cheap desks with hardly any interest in grammar. All he said was 'Go for it!' repeatedly or else 'Go for it, Bro!'

whatever that means I asked him to sit up straight and he said 'I haven't come yet, Bro!' I looked at the hot girl who was really enjoying herself and I asked her if she knew who'd discovered the Blue Mountains. I forget what happened after that. My memory fails me.

I guess I don't fit into the black system. It was a one-off.

My next job was at Struth North High School for a term teaching Creative Expression to country lads and their molls in Year Twelve. I wasn't billeted this time thank God and stayed at the Golden Noose Motel. It had very low walls so you couldn't hang yourself even if you were writing hundreds of reports. I dined upon microwave Baked Beans and Shepherd's Pie And Sauce and ate that on the desk watching the harness racing on the television set the night I got there. I forget who won and couldn't remember exactly what the function of horses was in the end. I think they drive you to sleep.

The kids were short on rooms in which to teach poetry or prose so the teacher in charge of me put a big white board in the hall and a fucked Texta and told me to do my stuff until morning break; I would have said morning tea myself. But it's called break today the same way a hangover is called a cold and teachers claim a sickie.

There were two hundred hot crushed children all bussed in from all over Struth. I looked at their IQs and wanted to go home.

So many kids looked bored and hungry and sweaty and unloved as though their selfish pricks of parents just left them at the school gate and went and had a big breakfast out and read the paper over glug bacon. They sat bored and mostly crosslegged on the lino as I drew Chief Sitting Bull with a stuffed black Texta and they followed along, drawing him step by step, some enjoying drawing, others screwing up their expensive paper and calling me rude names.

By morning tea they had drawn crocodiles hatching out of cartoon eggs by a creek somewhere friendly and many other pictures besides. I read back at my motel in North Struth and enjoyed the fall of the Roman Empire as recalled by an English academic born in Leicester where great cheese comes from. I love a decent Leicester on my tea table with a sharp knife in it. Talk about reward!

In my motel it occurred to me I wasn't lonely and possibly never had been because I am all child anyway and that is why I love teaching kids. They are spontaneously indifferent, cruel or besotted with you and you are to them the same creed. I've never wanted to grow up having met Premier Ted.

Fridays I'm never that good at and it must have felt a bit funny when our principal forced us to hold Christmas Day on Mount Stroganoff which is one of Struth's few geographical highlights. It is a very craggy grump precipice to be sure and on its top a wonderful inter-school cricket match was played eagerly with lady wicket keepers. After the batting and the bowling, the fielding and appeals that deafen you, a big picnic was organised by Graeme Simpson, the twin of Mr

Simpson our temporary headmaster. There was every conceivable food and dessert and the children tucked into baked yam and plum duff even though it was freezing and in August but so what!

Lots of leisurely teachers for a change enjoying a splendid nosh on really good scatter rugs and teachers guzzling scotch mixed with gin and kids getting wiped. The twin of the headmaster kept on, we sort of thought, you know, trying a bit too hard with the delicious cooking sort of thing, because he was all perspiration and intention, tempting the bursar with baba ganoush.

Fried alligator steaks not on too long. Turtle broth. Meringues and marvellous home brewed mead slavishly copied off Robin Hood's secret recipe book as told to Friar Tuck then somehow the school librarian made a copy then we were all devotees. About six the twin of the principal read us some of his unpublished book which was brilliant and had us all in tears then he ran fast off the cliff and killed himself.

We had to all pack up then and a few were more than put out. The principal obviously was inconsolable and poured brandy down his stomach all night after the geography teacher gave him a lift home on his pushbike, even though he didn't live anywhere near him and the bike had a front flat tyre and a fixed wheel on it.

'That's what occurs when you cannot get published,' said his crushed brother.

It was just such a mood change of the deceased brother. One second tending barbecue and dishing out serviettes and paper plates and presenting perfectly grilled chook and tossed salad including turnip if you don't mind. Seeing to everyone then reading a secret glimpse of his unpublished novel to much approbation of teachers and students all lying there on scatter rugs and cushions with a wine in their claw and a delicious cigarette to enjoy and then to leap off the pretty cliff after rejection from a publisher who hadn't even read a bit of it.

Saint Ursula's

I met with a gloomy Catholic School Principal at an even gloomier bar in the city and he said he was depressed with my resume. After that he left only to come back again like Lazarus and we ended up down by the Yarra River equally down in the dumps staring at incoherent swans trying to bump their heads into sludgy oil barrels. It was a pretty normal night but he just kept on staying with me, I can't say why, and in the end we sort of got on, we even liked one another and we were roughly the same age. Older than Time.

I forgot his Christian name and his surname and was just staring hard into him trying to remember why we were there, like a couple of tramps waiting for their Irish author to turn up, or whether Samuel Beckett ever turned up or sent a beautiful inexplicable boy.

'It's getting harder each day in Catholic schools to preserve people like you, whoever you happen to be, because data is all that is bowed to and programmed and finally worshipped these days. I have committed to my memory several of your stage plays as well as your poems published in the TAFE system, which negates their eventual study since poetry doesn't cut it in The TAFE System.' He threw one of his own socks in the river.

'I wished you'd come across to us and feel worse,' said he, with a suitably suicidal face. 'Anyone can feel perpetually bad,' he sniggered and lit up some Ice. He got high straight away and offered me a drag but I'd given up smoking five minutes earlier. He smiled and put his rough-hewn arm round my bull neck. I am particularly fond of my athletic neck and I suppose it has stood me in good stead since my early years when I realised I was built in a Herculean sort of way. albeit with a pot stomach that I'd had since I started to drink, at twelve.

He was a Colossus of a guy and a nose on him like a pig's vast snout and he practically 'oinked' whenever he laughed and he seemed to laugh just all the time we philosophised upon the foul riverbank. I could smell people getting murdered, the night air was so sweet and light.

We hadn't been drinking or swearing but somewhere in between we enjoyed what the other being was saying, about the chronic need for Catholic children to be funnier, to do away with a motor neurone Mother Mary, to quit guilt as the path to education because it obviously makes the recipient feel worse.

He offered me a year at his high school which is Saint Ursula's in Hawthorn and we shook paws eagerly on it. He told me I'd have carte blanche where their library was concerned and he'd set up my study permanently there with a big walnut desk and official receipt books, pens and ink and a suicidal secretary named Robyn Lockwood who had partly understood *The Pilgrim's Progress* and I had to state that she was a better scholar than I was.

He contradicted that and declared that no one was better or brighter than I am. I just wished I could remember where we'd collided, that was all. My memory was getting faulty with cask wine, although I'd cut back to almost none lately, whatever lately means. He tucked in his vast crumpled stomachs and fiddled with his fly to make sure he hadn't urinated unexpectedly, then amazingly he stood up and I heard his vast cruciates crack. He had wee little piggy happy eyes and his jowls sagged and shook as we made our historical way back to Young And Jackson's Hotel in Swanston Street, home of all male Catholic school principals. We drank all night in the upstairs bar and he shouted me a steak that came with its own axe.

I realised I hadn't been feeding myself since divorce came through and really enjoyed a prime cut with a guy who made me roar with laughter, so much so I nearly choked on my magnificent gristle which he reached over and gulped.

He gave me fourteen stiff hard Saint Ursula's taxi vouchers; you can't give a writer more in Melbourne, and I felt pride come back to my flogged hide. I drank wine all the way home then got in the bath and dehydrated only to roughly towel myself down and fall unconscious in a split second. I dressed a second later in a three-piece suit I'd given fifty cents for at Savers, although the legs were a bit long actually, so I had to frigging pin them.

I breakfasted on fillet steak at seven in the morning and whilst I got into it I popped some hay fever eye rinse into my bright sore eyes that had got much worse since my lawn got to ten foot high. I answered the phone to a friendly girl I'd met in an art supply store who possessed the kindest eyes I've ever looked for the answers in. I think I love her, in fact I know I do. She said she wanted to drop over that night to see me and my heart raced like crazy, even at 62.

I got a cab to the new Mick school and joined in the Holy Communion and mumbled my phoney Rosaries just to try and look 'in'. I was so splendid to behold in my posh suit and Savers OpShop jocks and tie that to me looked Catholic it was so forlorn. I got into a heck of a lot of bother at my first Double English when, racing along the slippery hall-linoleum I looked up aghast at what I took to be a Catholic school clock that read ten minutes to two and that would've meant I was late for the lesson, I didn't want a bad start on day one, but it was really a carved Cubist Christ with long and attenuated arms dangling over the barbaric cross. It just looked like ten-to-two the way they had it there.

I went in to bored middle class girls of twelve with impressive busts who blew revolting pink bubble gum at me. The teacher who managed the room had no authority over any of them and started screaming at them and displaying green detention cards at them to start behaving themselves and to afford me some respect.

'Good morning ladies, today we look at alliteration,' I began politely but they just laughed at me and slumped hard in their slapstick seats. I felt as though I were in a vaudeville sketch about illiteracy and that ended with death and unemployment as a climax.

I tried to write some verse on the white board but the new fangled electronic marker didn't come on and they just about pissed themselves. The class had been on less than one minute when my assistant fled the room in a torrent of snot and tears. I turned round and told them not to chuck metallic pencil sharpeners at one another. I informed them I'd seen a girl once lose her eyeball because of that.

They screamed at me like hissing ganders and they stood up in their desks. 'What fucking school did that happen at you fat dud?' I told them it was a long time ago, possibly in Swan Hill and they threw school bags and chairs my way. I pressed on regardless.

I was out the front and had got the marker going and and and – I don't know why I'm stuttering even though I'm writing – the pressure the girls were putting on me – I could feel my blood pressure rising and my brain go black – they hated learning, they detested Mother Mary; they intended her name change to Mother Maudlin. I suppose I panicked and tried seeing them for what they really were. Prostitutes.

They surged at me and mocked me. It was really happening and not a figment of my over heated imagination, they came rushing at me, there were an army of them and laughingly they tore at my hair and hit my poor face and spat most vehemently at me. They took off their clothes and dry-humped me.

I commenced weeping but they had other horrors in store, worse ones than imaginable. They chanted the Rosary but it was in Thai.

It got to a bit of an impasse I have to say after the fifth period when the girls had a nervous Casual Relieving Teacher assist me in sharpening up their grammar. We had to obviously change rooms in the sense that they had trashed the earlier one and reduced it to smouldering floorboards and skulls.

The new room was in the gym and I had to try to reassure the teacher working with me we'd make it out of there alive, but he didn't seem so sure of that weak hope at all. The gym was insufferably warm as though it were a spa kind of thing, and besides that it wasn't long before tubby blaspheming girls were swinging from Roman Rings and biting each other's rude bits.

I tried to look manly as I confronted the large instruction board out the front of a hundred wonky bleachers with either one leg to them or their seats incinerated by billions of stabbed cigarette butts. This time I had a pretty decent blackboard marker and for once it had some ink in it so I wrote a verse in it inspired from a lovely verse by William Blake to do with the premature deaths of boy chimney sweepers. They cast old plums at us out the front and brayed like beasts of burden. It felt like encouraging Blake to The Dead, for that is how they seemed. Dead.

The fat bitches in the front hurled their vandalised seats at us and the ones immediately behind those spat and gave the finger and swore so loudly my companion wept and had to excuse himself claiming a terrible headache as well as unbelievable delirium and nausea that only ends when you leave somewhere awful.

The great big German guy I'd met before with the detention tickets came in only to be randomly assaulted at knife-point. I just kept on writing verses up there on the board and hoped it's to end sooner than soon, like right now let us say.

The German guy was being ground into the burning boards of the gym and complained of being tired after thirty girls had assaulted him. He asked me if I'd ever worked in a Catholic High School before and I said that I had but that this one took the proverbial caraway seed cake. I'd never seen an unwilling German teacher assaulted by girls before.

The girls locked all the gym doors and set everything on fire including the old wooden framed blackboard I'd covered with Blake poetry. The German guy hobbled off to Sick Bay and I don't believe ever taught again or was seen again.

The girls loomed at me with yards of mascara on their beady eyes and hair dyed bottle-black and breasts either hanging out of their torn dresses or having coarse graffiti printed over them with my blackboard marker. They screamed swear words at me about education being bullshit until I had a bad headache. Then the bell went and I had to meet the parents in the staff lounge.

Their parents had even worse manners, for example one of the arrogant fathers, no doubt an I.T. Guy or a Range Rover salesman, handed me a volcanic overflowing black coffee in a mug, that as I lifted it from his grasp succeeded in scalding my lips and I cried out in pain. 'Get this caffeine into you, you moron!' he chuckled and sipped his one, not nearly so hot and glared with hate at me. His suit would cost more than I'd earned all my life correcting poor spelling. He looked like a Violet Crumble Bar.

'What do you think of our Debbie, you educational son-of-a-bitch. Do you believe she's got the right gear to join the Air Force and serve her country with distinction in Afghanistan in our war against terror?' His wife gargled at me which was like a terrier experiencing a brief blackout or a partial stroke, she had so much perfume caked on her old hide she nearly made me swoon

'Is she the girl who assaulted the teacher at knifepoint earlier today and then choreographed the burning of our gym?'

'Sounds just like her,' laughed the mother, concentrating on cleaning up her cheese cake and imitation whipped cream, which she appeared to see her husband in, for she addressed her next question to the cream rather than the man, and spoke in an uneven undertone. 'Why do we live, why do we bother with bullshit teachers when the world is our unshucked oyster?'

I told them their child was a pig and half hoped or even expected them to brain me for that remark, but it seemed to greatly pacify them for they cooed like homing pigeons and the father nudged me with his big head on my shoulder and said I was truthful, even though I was an idiot.

The next parents toiled as child psychiatrists and confessed their girl had only one hope and that was to be accepted by the Taliban. They cheerfully informed me there was a branch of these particular terrorists in Glenferrie Road and so I thanked them for that.

But these were the affluent parents of Year 12 girls who just wanted fucking and terror, understandably. The next lot of parents were Chinese-Australians and invited me over for a formal dinner after the exhausting parent-teacher-interviews. They ran a dry cleaning shop in Hawthorn somewhere and I agreed to it at once for that very night, at 7pm, as I was fatigued by bachelor feeds for one at my hovel. Sao crackers and Channel Ten.

At their humble home they dished up short soup with aplomb and introduced me to their Mozart-playing-supersonic-daughter Ah How, who played as dazzlingly as she looked, which was like a Beijing Hot Dog.

'We arrive in Australia expecting fuck-all and were never disappointed,' said the exuberant Dad helping himself to Scotch and much ice. I had Chinese tea all night but the mother was trying to sing to me off-key and she too had been on the bottle. They offered me thirty bucks a week to give private grammar classes to their backward daughter who could only spell Milo because that was the only word she ever read on the tea table.

The next morning I got the Year Fours or Grade

Fours I should say in their Primary School, and it was chalk and cheese, the uncanny difference between the girl barbarians of yesterday and the infant poets of today. The gentle and energetic English Teacher was Mr Nice himself, Tim someone-or-other who was such a beaming fellow and filled with kindness for once.

He offered me his own personal cheese and chopped onion brown bread sandwich as soon as I got in his neat but friendly cluttered classroom which appeared lined with love and interesting poems written personally by the children. They'd heard of William Blake and knew he sang his songs of innocence to his exhausted wife who perpetually bore him babies as well as boiling the nappies in the laundry, where they lived above his tiny printing factory in London.

They had composed their own verses inspired by Blake and these they read to me in gentle but insistent juvenile voices that sounded like the word yes heard close after a bad day of endless no. I worked with these Catholic kids all term and was asked by the principal to let him baptise me but decided I was too heathen, and he got that all hurt look once more. In my lunch break I began to worship in their vast and blinding chapel and found comfort in the smell of people's souls in the much-sat-in ancient wooden pews where Christ seemed at least probable and perhaps my new friend?

It was stern-mouthed women ran the Catholic School System and ran it into the ground with their 'don't muck about with me' expressions. They had bodies tougher than Death and they networked the way decay networks in the sense that it will never cease linking gloom to Redemption. Their Jesus wasn't a boy who ever played cricket on the path with his mates, not once. Their Christ was sorry he was ever alive and enjoyed getting the bolts hit into every conceivable molecule of him on the bloodied and big board of Sorry Boss.

The Catholic ladies, what was fantastic about them in deference to their pale imitators – the men – was their chronic ability to sack any woman who didn't grease to them and had the effrontery to show spine on the spot, the old black spot of 'know-your-place'. Jesus Christ of course knew His place. Clinical Depression. The Catholic Ladies lived in an unending fundraiser and guzzled claret quicker than Jacob's Creek could export it.

They were forever sending someone who didn't want to go there to Manila to view a hanging or to The Horn Of Africa to get hanged themselves on behalf of the angels in the good book. They loved famine and were always dreaming of living in one that declined to conclude. They hated indecision and only screwed on top.

But at Saint Ursula's the Deputy Principal took time out to know me and we lunched most days with the diseased swans in the forecourt where the designers had placed a huge bronze reproduction of Rodin's *The Burghers Of Calais*, just to feel worse.

She spoke of Blake to me as though she were he and gave me such a back grounding of 18th-century London printing shops I felt overwhelmed and managed to convey that to her as we traded sandwiches and I dreamt honestly of kissing her though we were both old; not that it matters I suppose or hope. It's a lost world without love, I know that if I know nothing else, and it's true I know nothing much else than that. The Deputy loved me and I her and we leant each other Blake's books as a sign of affection. It really offended her Heads Of English whenever I was the guest of her office and she recited to me from any one of her beloved poets, with her kind eyes closed completely in the certain knowledge I was properly listening.

These middle order authorities sighed in their chairs and shuffled in their boredoms as I recited Whitman without missing a single syllable but never patronising my friend by adopting an accent to make my reading believable ,just as The Second Coming had to be made believable.

We had such a good time resting together, forever strolling about the tar-choked flower garden, praying for peace in Hawthorn because it has to start somewhere, praying for The Horn Of Africa to go away or at least to become disease-free like Hawthorn. It was a signal joy just to be together and munch a cheese and tomato roll together on a bench. She was patient with me and never pushed for a baptism not even on lay-by.

We always shook hands after our luncheons-on-the-grass but I always wished she'd kissed me passionately, maybe it's just the loneliness after divorce. I was stricken when the Catholic engagement concluded but the next job was real fun. Back to Boil Street Special School.

III

Boil Street Special School Revisited

The very millisecond I reenter the dreadful hall in Sickening Road I contract the mysterious virus diarrhoea harder than hard and almost canter to the staff loo in sheerest despair and desperation but The Mistress Of Urine has gone to Thailand on a junket and naturally enough taken with her the key to the men's loo so for a panicky second or so then it occurred to me to dart into the boy's one but it goes without saying that it was even more locked right up and padlocks round it than the staff loo so I had to get right behind the crumbling mortar and mortifying collapsed brickwork and hurriedly do wee upon my own boots with a great vaporising hiss bouncing off them of wee steam. I see The Mistress Or Urine again in my hallucinations upon six-week holiday in Thailand with the original men's staff loo key glittering round her young neck. She surfs with it dangling on her. Back In Brunswick no one may do wee wee because she's got it.

The old hall was once Wesleyan and gloomier than death by AIDS.

The clinically depressed staff are addicted to emailing reminders to themselves so when I turn up for work at

8am I invariably see them facebooking and emailing and text messaging one another over a hideous fawn plastic oval table piled high with old and brand new banana peel. In between the ceaseless emailing to personal computers only a foot away, so that they could easily look up at one another and make whatever point they wished to without the furious typing of silent plastic keyboards, even say 'hi'; but they prefer high technology to the sheer crudity of talk. Fair enough too.

The feeling to the ancient church school is need for detonation because it is replete with an unutterable sadness that is not so much human as education, an obsession with modernity where it is never for a teacher to lead the way or even suggest a thing in any sort of invisible way.

The hall boasts several sets of bronchial balustrades that are heavily shellacked so old much-varnished bullants are embedded in the glistening details of the groaning stairs ever upward where I teach each day in a coffin. It gloomily overlooks Sickening Road with an 1854 window a shattered inch thick the hue of lung disorder. It is kept open with a dirty yard broom thus it boasts airconditioning the year round. I hate it and teach here every single day.

In fact my dormitory room in which I teach was once the original first toilet invented I think by the late Thomas Crapper, at least his name is printed upon its giddying ceramic bowl. You defecate into a revolving enamel bucket-thing and somehow a weir comes into play and your bog is flushed out to Phillip Island.

In the miniature teaching-room there is a collapsed chair out the front where the teacher is abused eight hours of the working day then goes home. Every single thing here is seagull excrement because the only window is busted and the filthy birds get in and shit on everything including the teacher's frantically hacked Tip Top sandwiches which are as unvarying as each day that is a perfect tribute to nerve deafness. The pupils come in the room in a violent and vile way and slouch to such a degree in the seagull shit encrusted form they chuck their workbooks on they often fall right on the floor which is an inch thick of seagull manure solidified over the centuries of idiocy.

Upon my break I go over to the Post Office to part-pay my Optus account since they disconnected my telephone at home overnight. I pause to make a decent job of writing out a cheque for a hundred and try to communicate with the bitch at the desk who used to be a teacher. 'You can't pay this Optus bill because you don't have a bar code number on the bill.' Her teeth were like high tensile wire saying negative things to me. I showed her the top bit of the Optus Suspension Order and showed her the cheque-butt as well as my current driver's licence but she screamed at me point blank range and pointed to the now torn bill and said loud as loud 'You no understand English you fat prick?'

I muttered unto my white curly big beard, 'I just want my phone back on. I'm contrite that I have forgotten my bar code. I had it on the tram. Can't you connect me again, lady. I'll cut your grass once a fortnight if you do.'

I left and went and bought a revolting Vietnamese salad roll having to fight my way through an acre of teachers all practically starving. The lady used greasy tongs to load tomatoes that were inedible and frozen to putrid offshore cheese she pronounced as 'sheez' and then whacked on frozen purple onion a foot thick topped with her own hand which I ate.

People demanding tvs that never work, not once, in their language which is Turkish or Swiss. Why is the bought food we eat so awful? Who's to look after poor old us? Why does no one but my son love me? I looked into a cheap mirror out the front of a cheap jumper shop and my reflection showed a guy of fourteen stone with a pot gut and hay fever with white pubic hair you can't see. I look like a teacher of literature who lives without anyone around; my home's a hovel but my son likes it and I have installed a really nice cupboard in his bedroom and bought him a year ago an antique owl made of winking ceramic made in 1956 in New York because lots of television viewers were going crook about too much glare bounding off their sets and some genius invented owl lamps whose eyes take away that kind of annoying glare. Lou loves it.

I guess I felt, in short, lonely. I bought a few mandarins at the Italianate fruit emporium and wanted to share them with the new boy I was about to meet back at school, the one aged thirteen born with only one arm. I walked slowly back; I was surprised I wasn't booked for too slow a gait under Heaven. The hideous packed trams shuttled by to Boil Street with hundreds of commuters coated with boils.

It is the fag end of August and the weather is having a psychotic episode. I woke this morning simply freezing in my single bed-donated by an ex school principal and wondered just why I was so cold and then looking up and recalling that I'd switched the violent ceiling fan on when I hopped in about nine o'clock. I wore a thick white eiderdown over my normal eiderdown , which for some reason got a knot in it which cannot be kinked out. I tidied the slum and sat down and like a dog I gulped my heart attack capsules – there are ten of them – blood thinners as thick as after dinner mints. I blew my hay feverish nose a great deal into just-missing-me-passing semi trailers pounding along my corner street namely Boil Street, the most frantic intersection upon Earth.

Indeed and remarkably the concrete safe bit down the centre of Boil Street just on Sickening Road is so dangerous to cross to because the volume of the transports make it shake apart so that when you stand on it clutching cheap plastic shopping bags with your kilo of mince and newspaper in, the whole thing vibrates. Very easy therefore to tumble into a vast and doomed cattle truck and be brayed to instant oblivion.

It is now and that means of course it is eleven and time in the room for a long English Double. Eighty minutes of insults, rudeness and body odour. Not that I can talk. I still haven't bought a washing machine for my rental property three years after divorce. I buy stuff at Savers and wear it till it disintegrates like hope of a new woman.

Into the tiny stuffy room the Year 10s stampede and as usual kick and hurl their great bags about; you have to keep your nerve when you're a teacher and sudden nasty shocking noises must be not merely anticipated but in a way, loved, because the kids live in a racket all their own. The sonic boom of single parents weeping each to each across all cities upon Earth.

Louise my supervisor screams back at the zoo-like kids who resemble mandrills. She screams to me and I scream back the lines of street dialogue I offer as a precedent; all they have to do is copy my lines down by pen or carving knife in their exercise books and add to them to complete the scene for our review. Some don't even try and tell Louise to go fuck herself. I have already been told that by virtue of their seething eyes as they regretfully come in.

It is chaos of course with Dean the thin illiterate boy diving again down into the safe confines of his stinky parachute top with the silver gaffer tape stitching on its base, which is where he keeps his head. He forms a foetal position as he always does in his own frightful garment and from within it we hear plain as day 'I'm not doin' this shit!'

I concentrate upon Phillip the boy born with a defect which is not having a left arm, just a stump is all there is; he clings to his personal computer with this and opens its lid to do his work or scratch his beautiful and noble head, and do all the millions of things all boys can do with two arms. He appears quite relaxed and jovial as we begin the writing of new light-hearted dialogue for the morning. He even shakes his head with mirth and disbelief at the novelty of what comedy he's written in no time. It's effortless for Phillip. He's a natural clown whose face looks like a Raphael charcoal drawing unseen unless you're a monk.

'Gee, this is so fun!,' he laughs and a few in the class are rolling about listening to the way Phillip reads his writing out to them. 'You're a good writer,' is exactly what I now say, then another kid signals my attention to hear him read out his new sentences so I cross the tiny room to her. She is funny and I laugh out loud the way she read the work, making really good accents for her characters. She has the class in stitches.

Then suddenly Phillip has a mood swing because he's not getting star treatment and proceeds to assault his own face, his beautiful forehead, that noble visage from Leonardo's secret sketchbook, he now bashes the froth out of his face onto the lid of his own desk. It is surreal to witness him repeatedly bashing his own dear sweet face in a state of mania into his workbench because he had to bear the ignominy of someone else's praise. I said to him as he did it, 'Don't you dare harm yourself. That is a very cruel and stupid thing to do to yourself. Stop doing it at once!' He then was led out of the room by his supervisor who gave him detention. He turned around at the door, pointed at me and screamed 'I'll kill you!'

At that I couldn't dream up a single comment. I'm usually pretty quick on my feet but there was something so tragic and awful about what I'd just seen him do to himself right in front of me. As his footsteps retreated away into the cloud of time-passing I unexpectedly felt ancient. He was enjoying it, I thought. He is a very clever thirteen-year-old. Why did he go strange? Only the local pharmacist knows the answer to that.

The day went on very slowly and I did my best but pretty much failed my own ideals of teaching. These poor kids just don't want to learn grammar or enjoy English, which is our language, mostly, apart from swearing.

Later is later and I am cooking pasta for my young son and myself. He is the same age as Phillip. He is so peaceful and calm as a cucumber.

He does his homework whilst joking with me after dinner; he sometimes to be cosy climbs into his new sleeping bag and puts the hood over his ears to keep them warm and does his homework on his own bed in his bedroom. He is beautiful looking, slim but strong and is still growing at sixteen-and-a-half years. He wanders out and we have a game or two of checkers in front of the television with the New York owl next to it, beaming away any glare to make our eyes sore, and so on.

My big treat each or most nights is to light a candle in a candelabra in the appalling bathroom and run the hot hoping the 'suss' boiler won't give the game away. It is a Paleolithic Rheem Hot Water Service that sometimes, if it's in a sulk, cuts out and I must bathe in tepid, if that, water. But if it's in a good mood it comes out really hot, in fact volcanic and I can soak away all the day's swearing.

I love to lie in the hot and observe peace in the springtime flickering candles in my cup in the worst bathroom ever undetonated. The old boiler reluctantly coughs behind its hand and fills up the tub with heavenly hot and after half an hour I cannot see the self-harmers of Boil Street. But in my nightmares I sometimes see them. Belting themselves up because it's all got too tough alone.

As I luxuriate in my rental bath my contented son completes his English assignment, which is pretty tricky; he has to write an acceptance to a dinner party in the style of Lady Bracknell. He has had a look at Oscar Wilde and figured it wasn't hard to write like that, and so I actually witnessed my clever son sit at his computer and write precisely like Lady Bracknell in nothing flat and then I remembered in the sudsy tub the so-effortless way that Phillip had written at Boil Street.

Why Exactly it is that Weekends are Worse for Teachers

Last Saturday I let myself down and drank largely white wine and chainsmoked out the back in my ten-foot-high couch-grass unkempt backyard waiting patiently for a very handsome theatre director to come to dinner expertly prepared by myself dead drunk at 7pm. She looked like a new bottle of white as she shimmered in and smoked and joked at high speed. I cooked my favourite when-a-woman-comes-meal of cheesy macaroni with generous sizzled chunks of actual real salmon.

She ate it in a single snap and declared it delicious and I'd made the hovel nice and swept up my opshop clothes off the floor and generally more tidied until she came at the stroke of 7pm. Her boyfriend picked her up 90 minutes later as they'd arranged. When she left I felt like a fool which is of course exactly what I am.

I slept until 9am and the bath didn't come on hot as anticipated. I was invited to gaze at masterpieces in East Saint Kilda at 4pm so caught the train or was it tram and just about walked there.

A woman I am friendly with has spoken to the guy who once was the husband of one of her many daughters (can that be possible? I mean she talks that fast I hardly know what she's saying to me) and this particular daughter once bought a Brett Whiteley oil painting for about $350,000 but now at auction it would easily fetch two million. I wander to the incredible mansion and am shown up three levels of unobtainable masterpieces.

You greet a Magritte as you come in that is worth more than your immortal soul; you then stare utterly agog at Monet and Chagall and the rest until you are pooped. The billionaire who gently showed me the work was so demure and sweet-naturedly made me an espresso coffee which the lady and I sipped appreciatively and smiled at a lost Leonardo last seen in East Saint Kilda.

That was last Sunday in the late afternoon coming down off a terrifying hangover. As I got driven home I remembered tiny tinted photos of the day. The nearly being run over to death by the man in his driveway who informed me I could complete my mandarin and that he wouldn't be put out.

At some stage of the slow-motion day I felt precisely free like a tramp out of *Waiting For Godot* but more accurately like a tramp I have always been in 62 years of life, wandering everywhere uninvited and unwelcomed by everything but the kind old sun who in her way has always looked after me and let me into the great and small secret that she is your only real teacher. Sit up nice and straight and do your lessons, which are endless, as in the perfect respect for Beauty and Learning.

My son had a bad cold and came over last night and as per usual it was ennobling to see him, but he was hard to please I suppose because he's still spiralling up like a young elm tree, we are exactly the same height for poets in Australia. Five feet nine.

He had a frightful sputtering cough and it was really quite a bad bark that he kept on producing. At one stage, as we watched a mindless home renovation program upon Channel Ten, he requested a glass of water so I went to the kitchen tap and was as usual surprised that it turned on, I mean everything about my rented hovel is a form of surprise. A surprise for example that I find it upright each evening and still there first shot of a morning, Not a single dime has been spent on it since its invention in 1947. It creaks inconsolably at night and of a day shudders within its own crucified nail-holes.

I drive my son to his high school by 8.40 am and purchase him a giant tin of energy drink that looks like a torpedo; he downs in it satisfaction as we motor alongside morons in Nissans like our Nissan. He loves to crumple the Red Bull can up in his fist and cast it into the back with a ton of other crushed old energy drinks. I drop him outside a laundry near his school so that he doesn't have to suffer the embarrassment of other kids in his year detecting him in my catastrophic car filled with books of poetry mostly and millions of pairs of odd sox.

My weekend was abstract to say the least and it felt important not to dwell on general lostness but get into the new teaching day as readily as leaves come to twigs of trees. It is now Wednesday at Boil Street and I have been requested to give an account of the success or failure of the last month of dialogue writing in my dorm room because in October the school is presenting all the sketches as a play or review. I look at thirty teachers all uptight and superior around our awful fawn oval plastic school table where the bank of personal computers lie waiting to pounce.

At luncheon which sounds so extremely toffee-apple as though we are a rich school with a few Oxford Dons chucked in for good measure, I met a new teacher I'd worked with here 42 years ago called Warren. I recognised him immediately and as we casually deafened one another over a few rounds of air hockey the affection for him returned like a punch on the nose. It felt centuries back when we attended our exams together at the Melbourne State College in Grattan Street Carlton; it's still there but Japanese.

Warren was the life of the party and possessed a never-ending panache as well as dazzling looks that got him any sexually transmitted disease you could think of. He was gangly and eloquently spoken and wore bespoke jackets as his daddy was a tailor in Elgin Street. He was so spidery-thin and sure of himself in deference to the nervous middle-class students I hung out with. Kids who had heard the calling on high and wanted to irrigate deserts as soon as they awoke and attend the dire needs of ostracised camel dealers, newly arrived emigrant tyre-restorers from Iraq.

The student teachers had the best intentions in the world and devoured every publication on Classroom

Management. In fact back in 1970 when I started there was a magazine entitled *Classroom Management* that had a topless terrorist as its centrefold. I read it every issue.

Warren and I had a cheap bowel-churning meal in a bad cafe near the school that was run by depressed French Teachers who were all over Melbourne apparently. I ordered toast and soap thinking it was soup. I could've had a shave with it. Warren, looking more twenty than sixty, didn't mind.

'It's great to see you. I recall the time in Arnhem Land when the school sent us there by eight-ton sliding-door bus with hundreds of junkie Koori educators as well as black children who detested us and got drunk in Alice Springs as soon as we arrived and then sold the school bus for enough for a flagon of wine and a carton on smokes. That's got to be over forty years ago.'

It is I said and stared at his unstoppable beauty. He had no Botox but looked so youthful I felt ancient. He had no bags under his keen hawk-like eyes and didn't have any dandruff or baldness or bladder problem as he sipped a hundred teas but never got up, not once. But fixed me with those steely opticals of his. He wore an immaculate jacket and I could remember just how quick with a needle his tailor father was. He could sew a shroud while you waited, no problem.

'I studied law and took silk after I dropped out of our work experience that never ends. I couldn't bear the pretension of non-hippie left wing teachers whose excreta doesn't pong etcetera. In a way I missed teaching but found the cash very rewarding. I enjoyed the drama of High Court cases and the notoriety and incredible sex with mounted police ladies who are absolutely driven by gossip surrounding murder trials.'

The same old cocksureness that blew my mind right back. I asked Warren why he'd bothered to come back to something as boring as teaching class and he said he missed a challenge and that all that dreary courtroom procedure was killing his spirit off, right off he insisted and boy did he glare at me

Warren and I cooperated after lunch with the board's new plan of taking loads of quotations from the Year 7s about how our school had failed them. This session took place in the filthy chapel with pew after pew stuffed with insufferable children sneering at Warren and me and telling us how we'd been incompetent since conception, even earlier. It was a most muggy day in Brunswick, so humid the poisonous pâté had melted early within each cancerous salad bun flogged off by the Viet Cong.

People were literally fainting as they robbed each other in Glenlyon Road. The bookshops were evaporative and not even junkie rare book robbers went in to take a shit in the non-fiction section.

The kids all smelt worse than I do and that is saying a fair bit.

I am intending to buy and to install a decent secondhand washing machine from Sickening Road but I never seem to get round to it. At least I do my hair on my way to work at eight in the morning.

The kids looked even more resentful than normal; not that they're in any way normal. Black, black, all dressed down in depressing off shore black rayon T-shirts that only make you sweat more then cling like friendship to your awful sweaty back.

A parent who won Powerball last week invited Warren to stay with his egomaniacal kids for a week to see how the other half lives. Warren said he'd rather be on life support in Kew Junction in peak hour but nobody understood him.

'See the problem with you parents is that you live right off your kids here. You can't wait to interrogate them after the last bell. You have such boring days because you are basically dull, do you see?

'I have known you in your millions from time immemorial, wheeling your dreadfully slow and terribly expensive bicycles up and down meaningless Brunswick all the day and well into the night, pausing only to annoy an Armenian.

'You are so self-serving and pompous your entire morning is concerned with scrambled eggs on unleavened toast and being served fresh squeezed orange juice by a Jew in Johnston Street too, because a fair few of you live in mansions in Collingwood but scramble across busy and choked side streets to get to Coburg because it's somehow become fashionable, even necessary.

'But you lazy rich bastards are only putting undue pressure on your revolting kids! All you do is look Green as if that will save the fucking miserable planet! Riding nowhere on fifty thousand buck bikes around fucking Coburg is the very thing that will end the planet. Mother Earth cannot stand any more dull heterosexual husbands with teeth-bands in.

'With your idiotic crash helmets on and your Tony Abbott brains about to seize you are personally destroying Mother Earth!'

The parents were rather put-out at being spoken to in this manner and one of them went out to smoke and call his brother who ran the Hells Angels. A few mums called him an ingrate and left in a humpf.

I sat with him on the hot stone steps of the institution I both worshipped and spat on and it was so pleasant to listen to him speak of his own theories on advanced thinking, and he did not pong like me and as he joked and laughed I realised I had to change my domestic priorities asap.

The gloomy grandfather of the most unpleasant boy in Year 10 who was a practising Nazi and wore great massive spikes all over his much-booted-in head glared at me and I at him with some interest. Warren noticed us glaring.

'I taught that jerk 42 years ago. He was just impossible. I suppose his fucking grandson is in your class now?'

I nodded and wished the whole family could be gassed in Ballan.

Back in the olden teaching days the longed-for revolution turned up that encouraged us young illuminators to love children and earnestly listen to them better than their drugged parents ever could. It was inspirational work similar in spirit to perfect Christianity or purest altruism. But today is a lot later and there is a quite different spirit in the land. It's called Advantage.

The Epitome of Learning

I was four and raring to go of a family raring to get into the firing line of anything that moved, especially writing which was moving because our friendly father used to emerge from the great darkness like some sort of soothing quality of light from our old road then he'd bear with him the sagging cracked worn-down worn-right-out army issue Gladstone or Kit bag and deposit the job for the evening which was, after tea, we never called it dinner, to key hard metal leaden type on the kitchen table for instantaneous letterpress printing first thing the next morning.

He would come in all coated with Collies printing ink then have a spectacular scrub-up out in the washhouse where the big concrete trough was. I loved the trough. It was sturdy and ours and Mum used to rinse all the washing in it and through it; then Dad would energetically go 'whoosh-whoosh-whoosh!' and scrub his honest inky face clean and clear of ink that pumped our house's aorta valve. John sat right to me and Chris was a baby determinedly hopping into his bowl of freshly stewed apple that he then would defecate a second later into his new beaut blue poo-pot with a look of sheerest triumph and if to say 'Yes!'

Dad would lean on the fridge in the corner of the miniature kitchen, this is in the very early 50s, and John was about eight and I was about five let us say, and the impromptu reading was melliflous and assured and carried with it the undying message of the beauty of prose. Dad had this light-hearted bearing and light-hearted stance in respect of the casual reading and because she loved him Mum would listen too, and say something nice like 'That is well put, Len', before she attacked the Vesuvius of dirty plates in the gaping sink. 'In fact that is brilliantly put, Len!'

He might read to John and I for an entire chapter doing all of the hard characterisations contained within *Treasure Island*, such as Long John Silver, Jim Hawkins and even the sound of the ocean thousands of sea leagues away from Rathcown Road Reservoir where our cabin was. I see him today in this my memoirs of both being a teacher and everything that continually orbits my calling. He is so relaxed and relaxing therefore to be next to. He's not arrogant or showing off as we used to call giving a moment to someone's pleasure. He just loved literature and was our English teacher at the old home.

Out in the bungalow John is asthmatically asleep on the above bunk and scrunching up his sore sore eyes and sort of listening to the winter wind, but he's got a bad earache and so he says, 'I've had the wind-honestly!' I am endeavouring to re-read 'Uncle Scrooge' comics and am holding a torch upon Scrooge McDuck who in this particular line drawing is joyously diving into currency in Money Bin Number Two. I am laughing till I'm ill. John is wheezily saying 'It isn't that funny.' But it is! It is!

There is a great contentment in the house, a robust

feeling, an indefatigable zest for body and mind to have a go at anyone or anything, and when our loving father reads to my brother and me that feeling becomes like an animal publishing house. Joy is typeset.

John and I run each morning across the line to school, the line being the only railway line in existence between Princes Bridge and Reservoir; so we wake and rush to school carting our little green and white plastic lunch boxes stuffed with Kraft Cheddar Cheese sliced thick sandwiches on tomatoes Dad pulled from his own garden; Mum rapidly slices these in big circles and shakes Saxo Salt over them in a mound and declares, 'These will give you both plenty of go!'

We race each other across hopping grass frogs and optical illusion paddock dogs; we dodge the train stuffed full of scientifically depressed office workers heading off to add up loss; we tear into Reservoir State School, sign the register on a pen on a mesh chain and go straight into Grade One for me and Grade Four for John. All the kids wear fevered shorts with crumpled tops and just want to run all day. The girls are very beautiful or deceased-looking.

There are fifty kids in my Grade One which is titled One F. Miss Blackcurrant is reading us *John And Betty* and is saying 'Betty Can Jump!' But I can't see her doing it. Now it is writing-time and we employ blunt pencils to express our feelings on butcher paper. I do a not-bad drawing of the Epping train from memory and my associate Lionel Bullock prints the words 'Woo-woo!' in the cartoon smoke bubbles I've drawn.

Cut to Boil Street and the inner city ghosts of Year 6 are endeavouring to write 'get fucked!' using blunt pencils on the identical butcher paper we hated 60 years ago. They slouch differently to us back in 1950; they are so shagged-out-looking they can scarcely blaspheme. Their poor little lungs inhale then swear. They are old-looking and lonely-seeming; not that they'd ever admit that. It takes eighty minutes for them to print a couple of thoughts.

I love them I do admit whenever I see them try to do their work, not that I see it much. To see their minds concentrate, their little tongues stick out in a show of concentration, to see their skinny hands grip the blunt pencil hard enough to successfully write a swear word is uplifting and gratifying. Some of them have their concentrating faces pressed hard right on their work with the pencil steering along between literacy and heroin.

After school their dependent junkie fathers demand of them as they wiggle away so unsteadily pushing a stolen pram full of babies towards Savers to buy another jumper, 'How did it go today, chief?'

They've completely forgotten their child's name.

You realise it is whilst children are concentrating that teaching is for you, it always was and always will be. They get it and in the getting is hope for a future that is something like a regular job; and not holding up Stop and Go signs for more hideous road mending. Sometimes, rare times admittedly the abuse lifts and dissolves into literacy because they suddenly understand the connection between the English alphabet and pride, even the previously un-dreamt-of possibility of a job, a home and healthy babies who can also write on butcher paper. Writing is a cheerful thing. It helps, like kissing.

The advantages of today are endless but they don't end with finite statistics as who is impoverished and who goes to a crummy school and who wears a bowler hat and attends Posh. It has to do with limitless income so that wealthy children practise boredom or Latin at Brighton Grammar School and really broke kids can only really hope for one lesson that should see them through life and that is sincerity.

I repair home and remember the longed-for-action of young kids eagerly writing, with me a prompter, me as go-between, me as friend-but-not-friend-just in my greatest friend which is writing. I check the mail for the usual ambush of domestic accounts that include (it must have been forged) a bill for $900 from Yarra Water. I have never stooped to sip it in my life, having once swum in it.

When my son isn't there I sometimes feel lonesome but honestly it isn't too bad these days. After fearing separation and going through divorce I suppose I am liberated but I sure miss someone to hold onto in the night. And living in a rented slum there is no pressure to renovate. You just go somewhere else as awful.

I sit after putting on the only gas jet, the rear left

thing that takes a thousand attempts to come on. Every night after school I get out my orange Bic cigarette lighter and say 'Fuck' repeatedly as I click it over and over and over as I hold the gas jet on like a moron to no effect.

I get hot tea going and sip it as hot as I can as I focus on my domestic accounts piled before me on the kitchen table, Water and Gas and Power and Car Insurance.

I get out my nice neat personal cheque book and hunt about for some unSoy-spilt-on-envelopes and take my time – I've got stacks of it – and make a neat job of writing out the cheques and licking the envelopes and putting stamps on each of them and sipping my idiotic hot tea. I have satisfied City Of Yarra and Vulcan Gas Company Pty Ltd and Vic Roads who are very hard to placate.

I wash my ageing face and wonder if anyone will ever love me again?

I have the friendliest face I've ever looked into except for my mother and father who wouldn't harm a blowie. I play the messages and one of them promises me a new contract for a book I wrote. My son wants to come over about six by Moreland tram. I fry some repellent tough buffalo steak slaughtered in a local church and then eat it on the floor. These days when alone I eat upon the carpet as I stare at the awful news bulletin on Channel Ten.

Last night I used an eight-dollar expensive new store-bought mapping pen to create a frontispiece for the new fairy book co-authored with my friend Jenny Lee. It was transporting to do that and maybe a hour went by without my head looking at the clock in the kitchen. Just tune in always to the thing at hand which in this case is drawing incredibly fine lines to make a picture so romantic book-lovers shall of course rush to buy it.

Learning so many things all at once when as a writer you please the book-buying public. You do signings and have lots in the bank. I find it actually easy to teach writing because I do that the same way my father talks to me in his tiny bedroom; I came in the other night and he was fast asleep and leaning exclusively upon his own left hard old elbow on his own writing desk, the one with the impressive glass top on it with an assortment, always neat to say the least, of pens and little things with the date of the year inserted in their crystal midst. He was out like a light with a grey and whitish halo of missing hair. He looked so weak.

He woke the second I stood beside him at his teacher's desk as it were and looked up with those beautiful big blue eyes of his and said 'Ah Barry! I had a dream about you last night and you were only a little kids of three – so happy and just running around!' He beamed at me and I beamed just being allowed to sit next to who gave me life.

He told me he was finishing off an autobiography by Clive James and laughingly quoted from it when he said to me, 'We used to have this dog that was so insane it used to run round our backyard trying to bite its own balls off!' He laughed until he was red in the face as in spontaneous happiness-combustion.

He groaned and sighed, whichever is the louder or both at once became unhappy as swiftly as he had just transformed from unconsciousness to joviality, and storytelling, then added 'I can't walk,' and rubbed his puffed-up legs and was obviously in agony; so I said 'Are you going to make an appointment, Dad, to see your doctor soon?' But he only groaned once more and I said I hope you've got Panadol. He is so old he seems transparent, just as my love is for him at all costs these or any days.

I then went into the heater-room where my sick old Mum sits all the day groaning for different reasons and my entirely amazing brother John comforts her from the second she wakes calling his name to the long long second when she is unconscious in front of the heater again at nearly midnight.

She focuses on me and says 'Tomatoes!' That means I have to go to the shops immediately to buy her some of them. It is a strange relationship. My tired-out older brother John is just about spent taking our ill mother to the loo and back, loo and back, loo and back 24 hours of the demented day. He waits patiently by the lavatory door resting his arm on the lid of the washing machine that has recently burst. 'Are you doing wee are you Mum?' he cries out from his permanent position of sentry.

'Nothing coming!' she replies and lurches back to

him at the toilet door that is always ajar. As she lurches all bent in half for some reason my brother stares into my eyes and he cries so hard he falls on me. I hug him so tight and as he sobs I repeatedly tell him he needs help from the council, but he obstinately declines that assistance. Is he immortal or something?

I go and buy fresh food for my old family so ill and worn to the veritable stumps. But it doesn't matter if I buy fresh cut steak John just sticks it in the freezer. Each night he cooks the identical dish for the three. Instant Poached Fish. Maybe it's terrific?

I always sleep and teach better after I've paid them a visit, although it can backfire. Sometimes I dream in rotation they are young again and playing tennis on the Sunday and Mum is roasting a fourquarter of lamb and Dad is standing by her making her roar with laughter and so on. My father's tireless legs stood the distance fifty years standing to attention feeding four printing machines on a concrete floor. He used to smoke in perfect beat to the pneumatic thump of those machines of his that kept the hungry family fed.

The Defeat Gene

At work today, a god-damned Tuesday, the unkind day in the week since Monday takes no prisoners after a weekend filled with longing and unfulfilled dreams that can be fuzzy enough in their own way to create in the dreamer the temporary sense of family, due to peaceful half hours all over the place, Tuesday is today and at 8am Brian our indefatigable preaching Principal is lecturing his staff on the latest educational theories upon a rogue gene called Defeat.

'Is is a particularly virulent toxic virus only recently discovered in America by educational scientists who themselves have only been recently discovered in America, surely a tautology. The rogue virus was hitherto thought to exist only in spawn excreted by mosquitoes that decline to bite white people. But I notice in this week's bulletin we receive from Washington online there is an entire feature story devoted to the uncontrollable contagion known euphemistically as Defeat Gene.'

A few staff lazily scratched their sex organs and reached for Greenie Coffee. Some were frantically yawning and others were pumping up their bicycles indoors and it's all right to do that if it's inclement outside which it invariably is. It rains in the fridge, I've seen that.

'The virus is an antibody in shape as well as intent. It comes when blacks move into the school and is never content until it bites unwanted tribes. When American woman conceive in public hospitals they bear very sick babies indeed who as they spread turn into teachers. There is no stopping this common phenomena and we in Sickening Road are soon to receive the mysterious infection because it just fucking comes. Any questions so far?'

Not one.

'The Defeat Gene it is understood in scientific circles started out in the era of Davy Crockett. Some of you Phys. Ed. teachers may have heard of Davy Crockett who was born in a coon-skin hat and got hanged whilst still alive by those rude people the Mexicans, of whom more later. Davy didn't really understand why he always experienced the emotion called "defeat" whenever his men lost to the marauding Mexicans who let's face facts were better warriors than the white scum Davy led. Mostly in them days backwoods persons were pretty good at Maths and thus their innumeracy didn't faze them much; they could count all the various living coons around them and point at a mountain near their crude ranch and nine times out of ten get its altitude right, then mark it off in their next important trigonometry exam.'

A few teachers out of boredom started playing air hockey.

'Now it is upsetting most of white settlement in America, this cruel and pervasive sickness that once it gets in your body never rests until you are dumb.

It stupefies everything in the head and that includes eyesight, hearing, sex drive and the crucial ability to defecate spontaneously, even if you're in an auntie's place with hardly any loo paper. We all know how that feels, don't we?'

A few more teachers join in the air hockey to make it a doubles match. They are de-camping.

'The notorious Defeat Gene gets even into the undergarments so that men cannot get them on or off without experiencing depression mixed with a foul smell. The gene attacks the body so that it can hardly get to the milk bar. It can't choose frozen peas or frozen carrots any longer. The new thinking is that it comes from inhaling chop chop Vietnamese smoking tobacco that you can get down at the market if you know a Cambodian or two.'

Some staff are getting so depressed they can't look at Brian any more and my mind is thinking of food because I forgot dinner and breakfast so I ask Deidre at Reception for the millionth time where the pantry is so I can do a thick peanut butter sandwich to keep me going. Deidre just points to something that sort of smells like instant coffee but could be a guy's shoe or his hairy epiglottis.

'The Defeat Gene is particularly prevalent in Sickening Road and whether it be new mozzies unscheduled and unheard of before we don't really know; the latest data we've just downloaded tells us these horrifying mosquitoes have sex in a sock and then bite a maths tutor hard in the side of the head; the result is insanity instantly with mozzies right through our airconditioning ducts.'

The air hockey game concludes with swearing as the teachers return to a talk that is only a bit better than the fucking game.

'Here is a blow-up of the defeat gene that Deidre just downloaded from America via the space dish located at Merri Creek. I will just bluetack it the blow-up to my own big head here, and with any sort of luck it will not sort of, you know what I mean, flap.'

The boredom of the staff is such that a woman media studies one vomits in the pantry and then asks me where the Panadol are but they are padlocked just like our loos. She lies prone on the pantry floor linoleum and I go over the hectic road to buy her some of my own Panadol. You always need them here and lately my work-headaches get so bad I swallow them at home. Out in horrid Sickening Road a brewery has big stallions carting beer in barrels with plumes on their insane manes and the unemployed throw fresh shit at it.

'This vile strain of course has put the kybosh on learning. Nobody learns anything these days that they don't already know. Another tautology! By gee how many have we got through this morning at our briefing! Be it a mozzie or be it sexually transmitted just like a rogue email the fact is that everybody bitten on the side of the neck by it has no energy to learn or remember where they are parked.'

He went on to mention it came as no real surprise for him to learn that many teachers had to go off for urgent one-on-one psychiatric counselling after or during morning parking because no one ever could think where the vehicle was so they either had to urgently develop a car-pool or try much harder to think where the car was. Some of them couldn't recall dressing that morning or what cereal they had for breakfast or quite likely it was toast.

'The bug it bites you in the glandular fever if it so wishes and after that it's all over Red Rover I'm afraid. It attacks the memory through the anus in Sickening Road which are everywhere, particularly if it's been raining. Have any of you noticed how much more unwanted rape there is in September?'

A few desultory palms sailed up but not for long.

'We have long suspected energy-loss may begin in the pantry which is the nerve centre of contemporary thinking or education; it has its young in the crunchy peanut butter so make certain you screw the lid back on properly to avoid this gruesome contaminant.'

The first period bell sounded at 11.30am and the kids gloomily filed up the stairs like death warmed up. I had the Grade Twos again but I mean they could've been the staff.

They looked fifty but bore contemporary haircuts so they were young, possibly, so I gave them a poem to compose based on the defeat gene that was going right through the hall. Astonishingly, they went to task and a kind of hesitant and false peace briefly reigned. My old hard heart it softened somewhat as I watched them actually writing things, with heads bowed and the filthy Sickening Road sun co-mingling with their nits.

I walked up behind each pupil and loved each in an entirely new way. They were lost and yet trying to compose a new sentence in English. They stank and yet they strove to butt up delightful words together to stunning effect. Their Housing Commission legs full of scabs and sores sat still and the rest of them wrote. They were learning about the old opiate. Thinking!

It was a colossal eighty minutes of quietly and inwardly expanding the old vocabulary of hope. The Oxford Shorter Dictionary Of Peace. I looked at their depleted bodies full of inquiry but not breakfast. The junkie mother chuckling at the idea as she hit up. The alcoholic father squandering the last grot of his change at the early opener; instead of straightening himself up and going cold turkey in order to cut his son a sandwich. The whole idea of nutrition just another gargle of cask.

The kids dutifully photocopied their poems then formed instantaneous editing and proofreading teams. Brian went down to Office Works to price the finished book of the kids' poems that would be launched by Barry Jones next May, he said. Maybe I shall teach here quite happily till I turn a hundred, I thought on the way home.

As I motored home along Sickening Road the ultimate goat track I noticed three mint-new large pharmacies

I'd not noticed yesterday. They traded right round the clock and boasted Indian arsehole security staff out the front with savage expressions sucking free Codral tablets and flexing their biceps at poor old passersby as if to say if you even think of pinching a Panadol I shall murder you!

The blur of rapidly pasted pharmaceutical advertising, the mop men receiving nil rest as they pasted the printed guarantees of everlasting life if you purchase offshore guinea pig capsules that fix the latest flus including defeat disorder. Customers gravitated towards the Indian chemist store bouncers like lovers and had their noses punched for them for getting too close to the toothpaste out the front for the black's liking; not that they ever liked anything but their pay which too was black so they didn't have to declare it.

I managed to drive poorly all the way back home, I can't say why that was. It had been a very good day and the kids had worked hard for a change, and there had been very little unrequested rape. The cars all went through change of life and became lost kids' faces to me as I freely hallucinated and wanted to cry for all kids who are denied an education, even if it's a shit one. I went and ran the bath because my body was hurting everywhere, but the boiler didn't like me again; it was in a mood and as a consequence didn't come on hot.

I sat in the filthy tub with my opshop candle flickering away with one inch of cold under my unworthy arse. The couch guy came who I'd bought the red sofa and club chairs from on the weekend. He kept on hassling me by asking, demanding how I was. I couldn't relate to him and just helped him get the new secondhand things in so I could rest myself. He laughed when he left when I'd told him I was a teacher. I went to bed unwashed and starving but feeling high because I'd witnessed kids doing it for themselves.

School Camp II

The Year Tens and I are down at Cowes near Phillip Island on school camp and it's a tempest.

For some obscure reason the humdrum wintry weather has altered into the wildest storm imaginable and the big flap-loving vinyl tent is protesting as wildly as the 500 miles-per-hour wind that is hurling itself through various black clouds absolutely stuffed with rain and big bits of bang-loving lightning. The other two teachers Deb and Robert have driven into the township to buy some food and soft drink. Come to think of it they've been gone for ages.

The kids aren't bored so far in that shrieking cyclones are nothing but a bore for them since they've yawned through so many DVD storms already and entire disappearances of towns and townsfolk, not to mention livestock such as entire cows are bullshit.

They are guzzling potato chips I bought discounted for a thousand bags of them at Coles in Barkly Square and the sound of the enormous crisps being snapped is quite tedious. They lie on their zip-up sleeping bags guzzling chips with the teenage-satisfying crunch to them as the crunch saves them having to speak to dick-brain teachers like us.

We have too many pupils to the cheap inflatable tent but I mean what can you do? What came first the chicken crisp or the tent?

In my exhaustion – I can't say why I am I just always am – I have completely forgotten all of the kids' names and they just blur into a giant chicken crisp. They watch soccer on Channel SBS and turn the volume up to just right for Year Ten which is chronic for the elderly teacher. The commercial breaks on SBS live soccer run for ten minutes every ten seconds or so it feels. With every conceivable item in life being flogged to you: tired hapless poor you at the receiving end of all transmission:

Bras for sexy babies and blocks of land for newly arrived immigrants.

Fifty hectare television screens and free mammoths.

The storm is getting much worse and all I do is pick up after the indolent pupils as they eagerly prostrate themselves into a perfect tableau of nothing. The wind is just about pulling my head off as I serve them up chicken crisps by stuttering candlelight that they keep on lighting because they just like stuff like that, you know.

Two girls are passionately kissing in the same fat sleeping bag so I don't have to see to them already. They are showing tremendous initiative. A boy is engaged in a brutal fist-fight with his brother, a kid called something or other, who wants to play footy for Collingwood after he turns twelve or so.

Mostly the kids are contented chewing junk food whilst the tempest howls away and now the portable television is out and so they can't watch SBS soccer.

One boy hits the television screen with an axe and they all sort of cheer him do that act. The tent blows off its stumps entirely and whisks into the sea to no cheers or sighs of boredom.

'Why did we come to this fuck of a place?' asks a gentle girl who is pregnant.

No one says anything but we all hold sopping-wet newspapers over our heads right on the cliff top and get an excellent view of Tasmania.

Some of us sit in my Honda and they immediately commence to smoke dope and pass around the scotch. I watch in dismay as my once real clean metal ashtray becomes full of vile stomped-out butts whose smell nauseates me deeply.

Two kids punch one another's heads in the back and I turn on the radio to see if they like ABC-FM Classical Music that is broadcasting Chopin. The child with the pneumatic-breast girlfriend who lives down his own parachute says to me 'I'm not doin' this shit!' I've heard that.

My old car is rocking in the wild gusts and I keep on checking the handbrake is on lest we all blow right off the cliff-face, but we do seem relatively okay.

Some kids jump off the cliff and others don't appear that interested in doing it as it's too much like agreeing to an activity.

The other teachers turn up and gather the kids up and have fetched with them hot chook. The kids sip hot billy tea and gnaw their fatty fowl and the vicious storm abates like a discarded dream. A sliding-door van has been booked and we all return to school like drowned rodents. Nothing was learnt about protection in the wilderness and the kids just went back with pneumonia, sort of thing, including me. We all coughed forlornly like billy goats on the way home to Coburg.

I lay in my bed all last night and coughed blood up either to my hand or saturated flat pillow like a length of slate, worthless slate you can't really get that cosy on, no matter how you writhe. I had to keep getting up to receive more off-shore loo paper from my stash of knocked-off school loo paper I proudly dispense from on top of my leaky lavatory, which is my real incubator.

I keep on trying to ignite my dud stove with a wet BIC lighter but all the dud jets they blow out and I swear like an old wolf under my breath and strive to get at least one jet operable again in order to sip some hot tea to drive out the bug.

I am shaking and sweating and doing the fandango in every aspect of my old body and realising if I die no one shall know; not only that but no one shall care. The rented slum will simply go on the market again and be leased to another male and divorced English teacher with no sex life or any savings. My heart is beating much too quickly. I can feel it panic of its own spiritual volition. My pacemaker needs two brand new Double A batteries. I have to sit up to cough successfully as my lungs hurt so much and that's the only way the muck comes up from the anchor of me.

I am so scared and all alone and the blackened heartless companion the night it never quits on me; it just continues forever and ever. Amen. It hurts to be unloved as my old friend Mathew the psychiatrist has said to me, 'Male loneliness post-divorce is worse than a psychotic episode.'

I sort of hallucinate on the stormy night with the blown-away tent and see the kids guzzling into their meaningful deafening crisps all the time because you don't have to talk with those in you. I want something, possibly Death, to come to me and hold me as never before in Her deep security, Her deepest concern that I am lost and cannot live alone without love properly. I would love to give into dearest Doom and find comfort in her bizarre skirts when the moon is really up in unfashionable Coburg North. Somehow I and the night are safe and we co-mingle and scrape through ten hours okay.

I dress and go to work and make great big thick strasbourg sandwiches with plenty of sauce on them with extra thick white bread to keep up my strength. I take my homework which is fresh-critiqued poems by the boy Darren who is getting his book printed in May next year by the school. I must have left the old Honda somewhere I cannot remember and catch the dirty tram up Sickening Road full of wogs.

The smell of a Turk's neck comes wafting up my sore nostrils and I wonder why they let them in, even Turkish English teachers decline to bathe. Two Italian ladies scream so loud about the cost of pork I have to move down the god-forsaken conveyance. I cannot remember who I am or where I'm going anymore.

Is this Coburg or Burn-Out?

I cannot hear anything any longer or even vaguely understand the stink of the tram, awful thing! People look like pigs meeting at a trough or just snouting around for something to do.

Why oh why do I stare into everyone's eyes the way I daily do?

Are we a brotherhood of teachers or hogs at trough?

The Carpet Shampoo Freak

This morning I remembered it was daylight saving so I put my mind back an hour and then I remembered you had to put it forward by one hour. At eight in the morning a terribly ugly little man screamed at my front door to let him to shampoo all my vinyl carpets; but I didn't hear him yell or push the front door buzzer because I was on the phone anyway. The guy on the phone was even ruder than the frustrated shampoo guy who kept on screaming to be let in. But I didn't feel like him.

After ten minutes of blood-curdling shrieking I undid the door to view him there with his great big impressive sudsing machine on wheels and his red hot face filled with hate of me even though I'm paying him $160.

We were not going to be friends, that was more than obvious in one glance at the look of him. He screamed one inch from me, 'I've been knocking for five minutes! Why don't you bother to open the door!'

He needed a shampoo himself his mind was so dirty. Where do you find polite carpet cleaners these days? On the phone his manager was also screaming at me the fact that he'd been knocking at my front door for five minutes. It sounded like a conspiracy or something. They were both so angry and yet the weather was perfectly delightful both indoors and out. All I could shout above his shouting was 'I've got the cash for you!' And that seemed to pacify him.

He plugged his gigantic machine in and started to shampoo Lou's room and then he did the other carpets in under thirty minutes for the vast sum of $160 which I got off the ATM in Sickening Road. The hate in him fled the moment he held the cash in his vile hand that needed hacking off.

I cleaned up in my way using a great big black ugly Gar Bag. I am so blind I couldn't tear its serrated top off and swore in my sunroom wishing he'd go away and shampoo elsewhere like on the moon. He glared hard at my paintings stuck on the walls with ducting tape as if I were a lunatic. I said defensively, 'I'm an art teacher.' The hate was manifest in his ugly eyes.

He went, paid. He was off somewhere else unfriendly to shampoo in hate for another $160. When he went I realised I pay $18,000 per year in rent for a hovel a squirrel wouldn't chew.

I'd be much better off in a paddock. Last week I part-paid $200 off on my $500 gas and power account because they had threatened me with disconnection over the phone. On the same phone Optus threatened me with disconnection if I didn't cough up $300 that day. No wonder men commit suicide when there's no one to help.

Having nutted out my personal style of teaching which is a cobbling-together of hundreds of influences based I suppose on the styles of lots of older teachers I have been mentored by and tormented by it felt a shock to slip badly today and have no clue whatsoever how to hold the interest of he Grade Fives from eight forty to morning play.

The second I came in the room today a boy slid down his trousers and lay under my desk out the front and masturbated but no one looked or cared in the least what he did. Two fat girls hauled off and biffed one another really hard in the arm with punching gloves borrowed from our gym. They made it impossible to get into the classroom and just punched the Christ out of one another. One girl's purple gumguard came out she was punched so hard by her classmate.

Many boys swung like mandrills from the smoky ceiling rafters and mooned me. I have never witnessed as many arseholes in my life.

Two girls tore up all my drawing paper, ripped it clean in two they did and then laughed a great deal over that destructive act. Gee, I hate wasted drawing paper!

It was a combined writing and drawing lesson but nothing got done but me. I got done in no small measure and was spat on at one stage and then ran downstairs to Reception to get assistance but the principal wasn't in. Judy from Reception said, 'They're probably a trifle down today. It's a long weekend and they're always a bit difficult on the following Monday as a rule.' She went in and kicked a fat girl repeatedly until her blaspheming stopped.

The room went a bit stiller and Judy glared at them and said if they played up again she's get a criminal friend in Brunswick to 'see to youse'. I went to the office and got more writing and sketching paper and started handing it around but they either drooled all on it or cast the dreadfully expensive paper right out the window on the top floor.

The youth who lives in the parachute said 'I'm not doin' this shit!' He sulked right down into the chasmlessness of his foul balloon pantaloons.

At recess today the deputy principal took me round the courtyard and junkies were staring stupid at the kind old sky for clues as to their next hit; he informed me how horrifying heroin addiction can be and that hanging out is certainly nothing to laugh at. 'Lots of drunkards laugh at junkies,' he added and I felt a bit queasy, actually. The sudden and so-swift truth does make you crook.

I sat in the shelter shed with several dirty filthy junkie parents and watched rats scamper over their needy knobbly knees like running and clawed malnutrition. These men were so much younger than me and looked so desperately ill I felt just terrible having scoffed at them often on my way to guts into a pie off the Vietnamese pie people. They were above all else my people, Australians like Julia Gillard. They were frightened and spectral and concave with lousy hair and track marks all over their hare-brained wrists. The ladies were mums of girls here who were sitting for their VCE exams. One glance at them and you couldn't hate them. I mentally pictured them moving in and them popping the couch I'd just bought for enough to score.

'We are trying to get the parents who use to learn grammar so it shall be simpler for them to apply for Sickness Benefits or any other thing to pay their rentals. We kind of saw you conducting some pro bono creative classes after school and on the weekend, not all weekends of course. We're not Gradgrind And Son!'

I said I would and realised by the knot in my gut that I definitely would do it. One of the mothers unfolded a drawing book with pretty cards pasted in. She said she was happy when she did that at her Catholic State School in the 60s.

'I'm the grandmother junkie mother of all mothers!' she cackled and I jumped. A guy told me he was getting treatment to give up junk that included poetry.

'Do you do complimentary poetry classes, do you mate?' he asked between craggy cheeks and blackened teeth. He looked just like a witch to me there, a real witch and not a line drawing of one in a book somewhere like a bookshop.

At nine that night I returned to conduct my first grammar lessons for the junkie parents of Year 9 kids. Brian sort of gave me a hand in that he kind of handed out fresh needles. He had to mind the office out the front of our school and one of his endless fascinations were Commander Telephone Systems, and like stamps he collected them in his office and loved to show them off to commercial travellers who usually called in for a free drink of water.

The drug-addict mums were making sense when

I came in and that was rare; maybe they'd not used today or maybe they had in order to pay attention to the mysteries of English.

They were old well before anyone's time, with over the top mascara broomed onto their bulging eyelids and foundation applied in a hurry so they appeared particularly rouged. They were mostly skeletal ladies as junkies mostly are and you could easily see all the track marks on their nearly invisible arms; many wore summer T-shirts even though we are in the midst of June, in other words, winter.

They wore exhaustion as you'd put on a much-loved favourite white soiled T-shirt. They all looked brutalised, which is heroin and crack's legacy. They looked so unloved in a way I was instantly attracted to them.

They all wore bare feet and I examined as if I were a doctor of ankles the chafing and thickened callus and damaged unbelievably ingrown bunched-up toenails of these determined women and wished I had the cash to shout them shoes from fashionable Lygon Street.

Their hair was big hair in that it was mostly wigs and you could see in a glance they had screwed them onto themselves in a rush because most were crooked and the effect was to make the old pupils look perfectly ridiculous or pathetic, which they were in all aspects in the deportment stakes. They wore cheap piled on revolting red lipstick, but then they had to do something to cheer themselves up. The men all looked like suicide.

They chainsmoked in our filthy tan bark and

cigarette-butt-infested courtyard and inhaled like I'd never seen men do it, with every cancer-hoping suck they didn't seem to be merrier, only more maudlin. Men Smoke Maudlin.

They were scrawny of buttock and vomitous of hair that was always tied up in a make-you-gag silvery pony tail containing bits of broken stubbie, bit of golden stubbie-top, dandruff, coagulated blood donated free of charge long ago by a friendly bouncer. They smelled bad, so bad. They wore opshop rags that never fitted anyone during a billion body swaps.

They too were bare-footed and some had sort of washed their footsies but most hadn't, possibly ever. The last wash they had was in the baby tub of their hospital when they were born junkies of other junkie mums and dads. Maybe Captain Cook used? Some people got bad habits directly from their DNA.

I got out the front in our chapel and looked at them until I could honestly see them unprejudiced. They all looked so sick to me and not just low energy but zero energy apart from the sustainability they got by chainsmoking and sucking on Diet Coke with lips like a squeezed-out old Wettex.

So we had about twenty parents from around Boil Street all together and I politely handed out sheets of writing paper and handed each pupil a Biro and Biro eraser because so many of them had requested one, maybe to eat.

I thanked them sincerely for bothering to come and

one of them groaned and told me not to patronise her. I immediately apologised not really knowing why that was but you have to have an even playing field in education, at least that was one of Brian's favourite catchcries.

I said, 'I hope you like literature as much as your children at Boil Street and that we are all eagerly looking forward to the review on soon where your own kids will strut their fabulous stuff. Tonight I am happy to introduce you to the world of the sonnet.' Two of them fell asleep precisely upon the mere mentioning of the word 'sonnet'.

They snored most loudly then fell upon the floor. No one minded so I got up on the old dusty church altar and wrote in longhand a couple of couplets that I just made up on the spot that were based on my love of nature, particularly ferns and waterfalls. To my surprise they all copywrote the two lines down at once and in the end they composed an additional twelve sentences to make a sonnet.

To view the night class of truly addicted-to-trouble citizens take the sonnet class so seriously and share their lines that often rhymed remarkably well; this just about blew my prejudiced mind. I realised how prejudiced my intelligence was as I studied the bedraggled group begin something they possibly wanted to try out, stumble a bit and then crane their necks over the writing pages.

They wrote in a way like their own kids did. The

tongue sticking out the side of the puzzled lips, the saying of words aloud, giving to their free expression an alchemy of thought that was now to be savoured, enjoyable as a hit.

I looked deep into them as I sat out the front and wondered what their home lives might be like. The sorts of mattresses they snoozed upon, the kinds of junk food junkies devour out of the other strong addiction to whimsy the kinds of household words their families shared and the quarrels. I have been witness many times to incredible arguments in the gaping gobs of housing commission flats.

The smashed and opshop dinner dishes re-glued and therefore perpetually ruined. The rotten teeth of addicts and their fecund breath. Their horrible food gobbled and thieved on the lope more than sprint for they are spent just about at the age of forty and cannot really be relied on to run anywhere except the congratulatory tombstone.

How hard it has to be to get off smack I thought as I stared at them writing away in all kinds of ways, slow, hesitant, apologetic, brilliant. So many of them were brilliant and wrote brilliantly given half a chance. Given a sheet of paper it wasn't that possible to smoke.

One lady addict came over to me out the front and put her claw on my leg and said I was cute. She showed me her sonnet which she'd co-authored with a guy who said the writing program at night was invented by Rembrandt.

It was a bit long that's all, the night class and by the time we'd shared our poems and I cleaned up the coffee saucers that they'd deployed as ashtrays – fair enough – then put the rubbish out the front of the school and the hardest bit is invariably to hear their home lives after school, the understandable whining and going crook about the cost of living, I didn't get home till really late.

I couldn't cease my cleaning when I got in and scoured the bathroom and scoured the grimy kitchen floor by kicking a filthy old stiff red beach towel across it with hot water – reasonably clean it was because I'd looked right in the plastic bucket – I did the dunny after that and guiltily replaced the toilet roll that only had one leaf on it left to wipe a guest's bottom with.

I bent down low like a supplicant under the oven and amazingly discovered the bit where it is very possible to gas oneself or put on a baby leg of spring lamb. I did the latter and went and studied my accounts on the avalanching tea table.

I sipped ti-tree tea and got out my faithful cheque book and pre-stamped envelopes and spent two hours hand-writing bills to energy companies such as SIZZLE-LOSS and NOT THERE ANYMORE.

I usually part-pay my domestic accounts and always feel smug whenever I insert a personal cheque for a fraction of the net worth of a pressing Optus bill. Last time Optus disconnected my phone it cost and arm and a leg to get it up and running again; as well as the phone getting cut off the messages don't record so your best friends just think you're dead.

I gave City Water two bucks this time towards a monumental bill of over a quarter of a million bucks or possibly I didn't read that right. I have the greatest trouble with my glasses. I pay two dollars at least for a single pair of them off the Chinese in Smith Street. But after reading anything the lenses fall out and the armatures go in your fucking ears. It happens every single time I read anything.

I didn't dine on the baby lamb as it turned out because I had a bath instead of eating anything. It was a very muggy night so I lay hot and crabby in my bed listening to the clinical depression of my electric fan to my left as well as the roaring of the fantastic overhead ceiling fan I use without fail every night.

I dreamt I wasn't lonely and was still married before my divorce came through. I dreamt I was being made love to by an American lady with teeth larger than a picket fence. I woke up and went to work.

The trip up Sickening Road was the worst traffic snarl I'd ever experienced, bar none, and I've been in heavy traffic 45 years, which was when I got my licence to feel awful amongst ten trillion lunatics who just want to murder one another. An Italian man in his eighties at least was ramming me and putting on his hazard lights and baring his teeth and swearing at me and showing me the magnificence of his considerable peasant fist. He probably worked in the field of rural agriculture in Italy before he migrated to Boil Street. A midwife for bulls, at least.

As he rammed my old bomb car over and over I contemplated what it should feel like to kill an Italian. Where I rent they are everywhere and all of them drive Valiants made in the sixties and ram Anglo-Saxons as soon as they arise until they expire after guzzling home-made grappa by the barrel and beating up their wives because they just feel like it.

But I am prejudiced. Serve me right to fall in love with one of them, a woman possibly and even a teacher, that'd do me fine. He repeat-rammed me and bounced into my door right near my tired-out head. I got out at Moreland Road and threatened him to a fist fight there on the spot. He just about soiled himself and I felt like a big shot.

Brian put me in with the Grade 4s today and some of them were bigger than me; and one had a worse pot gut than I have. He probably drinks pots at night with his old man, a hit man.

The kids were keen as mustard so we commenced operations writing poems that have to do with love and hatred; I urged them indeed to be candid and cutting with their new hate verses and light and playful with the love ones. I read them some poems by e e cummings that luckily they'd not heard before and I showed them my old curled copy of his poems and they could see how he was influenced not just by other poets but by the way the work was typeset. One kid called him a genius and another called me a cunt.

The kids were very proud of their 45-cent brand-new exercise books Brian had purchased from Office Works in Clifton Hill. If you buy a million books they chuck in one free, though it's not lined. After work I caught the city tram and caught pneumonia.

I couldn't cease my coughing and much sputtering until the bloody stuffy tram pulled up at stinking Princes Bridge, true home of racial prejudice. I watched the false Scotsman who's always there, pretending to be playing his bagpipes which aren't real and made of gaffa tape and old stick with a tape recorder inside the tartan bag he did by stealing a girl's skirt in Moorabbin. On the tape are piercing Scottish airs that are very awful on the earhole unless you happen to be Scottish, which no one is.

He had sixty bucks in shrapnel inside his saucepan at least and his cheeks were all puffed up as though he were really playing; he sweated something shocking and his red hairy bandy legs made me want to puke. I swept on to the Victorian Arts Centre and met Claire who I truly like.

She is dreadfully pretty and possesses a triumphant giggle and wears beautiful Indian stuff and smells nice. We took in a show called *The Europeans* and examined in minute detail the astonishing watercolours of two hundred Frenchmen. We nearly collided noses at the Fragonard. She spoke in the most nonchalant series of whispers and walked like a queen. I told her I have no expectations in terms of relationships and her eyes looked a bit disappointed, really, for they are very comic and dramatic, those amused and amusing therefore eyes of hers.

Outside the Arts Centre I said to her, so sweet and friendly to me there, 'Won't your husband be missing you by now?' She replied, 'No, not really. He meditates.' She reached either up or down then kissed me tenderly on my cheek or cheeks and I felt like making love to her; but it was just a nice moment.

As I walked home through my city I wondered what their home life is like? Does he climax or play darts? Does she love him because her swami instructed her to? What is love, really, when you get right down to it?

All through the city I trod just about on beggars and soiled lost bush children down on their luck in the big smoke. So begrimed and lost-looking they all were, someone's sons and daughters, come to Melbourne for the fun that isn't there any more, not once your money fizzles out.

I met a prostitute girl, at least she seemed like one and she was carrying a dirty dog with a red and gold sash attached to its neck and crying bitterly in Little Bourke Street. I asked her what was up and she explained that a thug had beat her up and used her up; she wasn't exactly sure she said which one of those was worse. I gave her a hundred from an ATM and she stared at me aghast.

I told her to get a room at once and to get in it. Get off the filthy and dangerous street, I added for good measure. Get something tasty to eat tonight and not junk food from a 7 Eleven, which is where half our country eats out.

I sat with a criminal for a time on the cool thrip-infested lawn of the State Library. He stretched out his so-long legs and I asked him what he going to do with the remainder of his day. 'If I tell you that I'll have to kill you,' he explained and lit his smoke. I liked him at once and he must've liked me back because he told me a sentence I'd never heard before in my life.

I began walking everywhere again, a thing I did all my life, now that I'm speaking as if I were deceased, far from it, but the daily round was always walking, perambulating isn't it called? The walking calmed me and comforted me and cooled my feverish and over-emotional make-up and with each stride I beheld once more the beautiful and odd faces in the particular streets and paddocks I strolled over.

My philosophy has always been people in all their moods and annoyances, carbuncles, anxieties, minor triumphs, heart attacks, births and bizarre heads. I have seen whomsoever I meet and immediately draw them, either as caricature or dead-set-real; and all of their voices are my education and lesson in humility, which is the most eager lesson in my racing heart, that organ of hopelessness and cheap betrayal.

I began after meeting the old jailbird to see that the way to teach for me was to shut my stupid fat mouth and faithfully listen unless it is a staff meeting upon a Friday evening and with the best intentions in the world

I know it's not for me and that I can't even pretend to absorb a single fact that they are bandying about. Christ Almighty died of facts.

I started to prepare my voice and heart for the lessons that I saw as lessons in life and never in Grammar or Literacy. I still adored typefaces now called fonts and I still loved to paragraph my essays and I honestly confess here to you that as a good and faithful servant of writing each day I used 'NP' that stood for 'New Paragraph' whenever I concluded a paragraph deemed worth preserving.

Maybe it stood for 'Not Pornography?' I couldn't tell some days, especially when the Grade Fours swore full-on, even worse than a pub on a baking hot day in Sickening Road where drunkards the hue of a rotten plum lean their crazed craniums out the front windows and bullhorn abuse onto tired pedestrians sizzling home in bubbling heat. Drunk men swear because they failed V.C.E.

Today it is now and I am encouraging Darren, who is twenty and has not got his VCE for some reason, possibly it is his epilepsy, which he controls and has written a brilliant paper on epilepsy according to Ray who is his class teacher and he should know, and besides Ray told me he's find that essay and lend it to me so I could read it for myself, and skinny housing commission Darren whizzes into Reception the same exact moment I come in to teach him.

He grins with his shovel-wide teeth that run parallel

to his head. He laughs just at the sight of me, which is the effect I sometimes have on people, otherwise I'm not sure what my position is with them; was I not placed on our blue planet to make them laugh? I believe I was but often I am not funny just as lots of men are not me. Maybe I should have been a slave to corporate greed? It's hard to say because you seem to get too close to yourself.

Darren has promised to keep a new diary but keeps on forgetting to obtain one. His mother who is brilliant like her son sometimes drives him to school but mostly he catches the train in from Thistle Meadows near Thomastown. Darren has fallen through the net. As they say, in all other schools and only Boil Street Special School will have him. The only other schools are prisons. There's actually a school entitled Pentridge Primary.

He is so skinny I can hear his lungs dilate. He is so thin I can't view him side-on. His body requires more maintenance or it shall not live. His hair is all over the shop and he never ever combs it or brushes those coal shovel teeth of his that resemble awful biscuits, that when he is talking, will snap right off as they grind on one another like a dental gearbox. I can hardly understand him.

We sit today in the screaming courtyard where tough kids belt one another in the middle of the back with anything that can be hurtled, including you if you are on yard duty. I give Darren a huge bag of Thailand Industrial Waste chocolate coated peanut brittle – I've done this a lot before I know that – but I can again overhear him tum-rumbling for want of food and prop the crinkly cheap bag of not-good-for-you junk food along to him.

He stares with drooling rapture at the glug and as his long thin fingers worry at the bag to get at its innards he says with a blurt 'You're trying to tempt me!' I laugh and admit that my only concern is that he continues to eat rather than drop off the twig. He hops into them as we read aloud his latest poem which is a dedication to his grandfather who died today; his father rang him on his mobile to tell him so and you can easily picture how tough that would be if it occurred to you as a twenty-year-old schoolboy-poet.

In a stammering but certain kind of voice he finds the pace, resonance and confidentiality you need to read aloud your new and secret sentences and traces every wobbly biro'd letter with the fault-finding-fingertip of his right hand and in a way it is or it seems like it is revelatory.

The poem is simple which is the hardest kind to compose and it is complex because each new sentence has to be just right and he invariably smiles in triumph when he gets to the completion of the new verse and looks deep into my eyes to check what I think of it. I think it is beautiful and can see that he is writing like William Blake again – not that he ever reads him.

But the new writing by this lonesome boy who is falling apart at the seams and has never got a cent to bless his hide with, who is always starving-hungry, who badly needs comfort but has that mostly from his doting mother, each word was his, they were writings and thoughts only his brain could process. Not the bad cheese of clichés.

I must have got slightly distracted in the noisome courtyard fuelled by blaspheming because for a second or so I fell completely asleep under the spell of his invigorating poems. He said, 'The spell broke when you looked at the mopoke.' I said to keep it in.

In the end he read several first-order poems aloud to me and Brian has promised he and I that the school will print them next year and have a launch: a thrilling prospect for an honest and anonymous bard on one Weet Bix a day.

I suggested that one day he may be a teacher and specialise in spiritual poems and he took two minutes exactly before he sputtered and gasped and said, 'That's not a bad idea. In fact it is revolutionary in several aspects.'

I can't imagine him doing his Dip. Ed. but maybe he could; not that I was any great shakes as a pupil because I only got 50% out of 100% at the State College a lifetime back.

I watched him have his equally thin Mum put her even thinner arms round her son and escort him back through Reception and out to the community sizzle Brian had organised at the very front of the school. I went out there just after them and saw recently released jailbirds forking sausages and shoving lots of sauce on each, burnt or not and selling them to the unsuspecting public for fifty cents each.

Lots of hungry poor were gathered round the three long pinewood trestles and stare famished at burnt fat. Was I hallucinating or did a dog put its hand in its back pocket and discover a buck in order to buy a hot sausage in a pool of sauce with blowies all through it?

Our Geography teacher sprayed insect repellent over everything and then smoked into the buns. Famous bisexual rubbish collectors bought burnt snags as well as modest booksellers who had decent sex.

I watched ravenous mother and son hoe into several cooked-perfect sausages that our hardworking principal personally cooked and handed over with a startlingly white serviette that Brian had pre-set in his breast pocket like a white folded fan of personal kindness. Kindness was on the school and at long legged last I was getting the Sandy Blight out of my cruel and jaded bloodshot eyes.

Today was like a dream starring listening. I decided not to lick my divorce-wounds, not to cruelly apportion blame upon my honest and hardworking former wife for having the wisdom to leave me. I saw that just waking up was miraculous in itself, of itself the sensation was gratitude far in me. My mind and my soul declared time out on bitterness and my fevered past was placed in a paddock.

What use is the poor old past anyway? All it does is

nip the bud of flowering hours that are love's gift to all who find themselves redeemed. All who have seen that loneliness is a present, a flourish, a magic that cancels tight-lipped hopelessness – the lover of darling despair!

I worked hard at being more thoughtful about my entrances and exits at the school, not to treat the staff like human boot-scrapes and shut my stupid mouth and start to learn teaching from two of the social workers there. They had no time for sensitivity or talking up or down to the skinny and fat children placed in their care. I observed just how quick they were to grab the seconds of each fleeting minute lest the kids thwart their exams.

Today belongs to the exquisite attention and gumption kids require so books that aren't important become holy writ to them. I dug hard the stubborn wax out of my spoiled ears and started to hear the things the two social workers began to say to Year Ten children, the way they spontaneously spoke and that the choosing of the exact word of encouragement got through to sleepy highrise children who hadn't had any breakfast, didn't possess any roll for their lunch and stayed starving practically all the day at school until Brian fed them himself.

Brian set up old trestle table and went to his battered car and returned time and time again with things like fresh pineapples, curly and terribly costly firm but semi-circular bananas, clusters of transparent grapes full of Vitamin D I'm informed. And to see our leader, tireless principal place these scrumptious fruits for the starving pupils on the old pinewood fold-up trestle really lifted my heart, the heart of mine that was so troubled and in a way didn't deserve to work.

I was for a short time beginning to see our school as revolutionary and although I loathed clichés I started chatting to fellow teachers about working 'at the coal face', as if you were a miner all the day. I started to fetch in fruitcakes I baked at my rental property and served each up sliced to a teacher each. No one one ate any. Nary a crumb. I picked at my bit on the tram home. I even gave a chunk to a ticket-examiner. He chucked it out of the tram.

As if high upon drugs I started to not merely see each teacher differently, almost like a work of art or a poem, possibly a jazz poem, unique as a cloud of assorted and undefinable words, a speaking vortex but I began to see everything for what it was and not something my cynicism made of it, or my depression made of it. The hideous became an alchemy that transformed a stupid tram driver into a wise man.

The impossibly cruel and taunting pupils who called me 'brain-impaired' became my loved ones. When they spat upon me I adored them. It was from my childhood version of truest Christianity formed at the local Baptist church where morons instructed me in the power of misery and the mysticism of crucifixion. They said that Christ was nice. But he never looked that nice to me when I was a little boy enduring the paranoia of kindergarten. He looked awful.

If the kids slagged on my shoes as I came in over the

boot-scraper I forgave them wholeheartedly. I blessed them whenever they called me a rude word. I bent over so willingly to pick up their broken pencils which they busted deliberately in order not to learn English. If they came forth and screamed at me I smiled like a fool into their deranged midst. I held their illiterate pencil and showed them how to spell Chiko Roll.

At recess I commenced to tune into the right way of speaking when the teachers sipped their coffees and nibbled their doughnuts sprinkled with catch-cries. I started to understand their jargon and imitated the sound of things like 'one on one', which clearly stood for talking to one person and closing your mouth.

I washed by hand my filthy navy blue singlet the thing I slept in and smelt better at Morning Conference. I rinsed my hair with dog soap of a night even if the old boiler didn't pump out the hot. I came into work with a new attitude.

I saw the light, brother.

It hurt one night, hurt hard when my Honda Civic was thieved. It got knocked off outside my place and in the morn all was left was oil spots and its former shadow. Not even a note to say sorry about that. I commenced to hate my Coburg back street in a new way. It was at least forty years since a car of mine was knocked off and it couldn't have come at a worse time. Why does the theft of your car hurt more than the crucifixion of Jesus Christ?

At recess I rang Brunswick C.I.B and just getting

through to a copper who'd listen took twenty minutes. He couldn't have given a stuff that my Honda was gone; I could just tell by the boredom and sarcasm in his smoker's cough. He told me it had been found and was at the Moreland Council Pound For Thieved Cars And Trucks in Boil Street. I rang them.

After work I went up there and a guy, quite amicable, checked out my registration number with their huge database of pinched other Honda Civics. He said it was a hundred miles out of the CBD at this remote pound near the Werribee Zoo. That's where all the giraffes are isn't it? He kept appearing and disappearing in this tiny doorway of the council all the time and charging up several flights of carpeted stairs to re-look at his data base.

'Bit of bad luck,' he yelled as he rushed into view again, holding the crucial information pertinent to the pinched car. 'It has very sadly been set fire to in Dandenong by a sociopath.' Fair enough I replied and that was the stone end of that.

That was a false call though and in fact my car had been pinched by persons unknown and set fire to in Coburg where I rent, in a street not far from the slum I live in.

A lady known as Anastasia from Thieved Cars who toiled for The RACV rang one night to assure me it had been incinerated but never to mind because it had comprehensive insurance on it part-paid by me once a month when I have bill night at my joint. I have a bath then sit down to hot tea and pressing accounts.

It is turn-on for me to hand-do my urgent bills by human cheque book and whack the 60 cent stamps on the offshore envelopes then post the stupid things so my house isn't removed from my old body one night when I least expect it. Mostly I part-pay due to the solemn fact that the money they pay us isn't enough to live on.

What I mean is enough to live on? The real estate Goebells I pay rent to telephone me all the time, demanding I pay by human cheque one dollar to them because last time I paid my monthly rent I was inadvertently a buck short.

Now the weeds are around the roof they are so high and gorgeous; and as I get chronic hay fever from all grass I decline to have anything to do with them; and just see them through the window each evening behind the telly, swaying big as palm trees or untreated female hernias.

The real estate moron keeps insisting on my paying a gardener to slash them back, but I keep forgetting. The other night I was suitably shocked, even traumatised by the baffling apparitions of him in all his Italian morbidity standing there superior in his corrugated three-piece suit and bullshit lime tie with his idiotic vinyl clipboard and the freak landlady who once lived here before it went to ruin.

They were conferring in the sunroom, I could hear their Capitalism. I stepped into the laundry to confront their superiority and the landlady confessed to me she was heartbroken to see the place not weeded and the lawn higher than the spouting. I pointed out that the boiler didn't work and that only last night I had a cold bath. She said she couldn't make the connection.

The guy wrote to me last week stating he would send one of their zombie gardeners round with a state of the art mower and slasher and it would be on me. I would rather pay The Devil to give me a punt down the river Styx.

A Particularly Difficult Girl

Today she is again there in all her beastly snideness and super bra. She is a year ten heathen bitch whose crazed grandmother I taught here 39 years ago before the cops shot her in an armed hold-up in Moreland Road when she stuck up a butcher shop with a tomahawk and grenade.

This awful child is dressed in military fatigues with a toy plastic rifle round her bottom. She has been seen smoking crack in the computer room and was given detention of twenty minutes for kicking a Prep. She is stoned and drunken and her lecherous boyfriends ogle her ample bosoms as I come in to talk to them about assonance.

The small tutorial room is set up like an impromptu science laboratory and Mr Richards has been teaching them about bats and why they defecate entirely upside down in our botanical gardens. Several bat skeletons lie on his desk.

She has such heavy eye make-up on it's hard to see her at first. She has her big heavy breasts resting on her pencil case which is bowing under the weight of them; in fact some of the pencils are broken.

A drugged boy is smelling her bottom as I head towards the desk out the front. Another stoned admirer is kissing her pimply neck and yet another is ravishing her sandwiches.

Her big boots are resting on her desk and they have both been just stamped hard into filthy crumpled pizza lids with dog manure embedded into each and these are held up for inspection; the smell is completely atrocious because I know the particular dogs that shat on them.

She is laughing her head off at the sight of me coming in the room, an old man with a big white beard and baggy eyes, very baggy sore eyes from a lifetime of chronic hay fever for which there is no cure, and she is now all red in the face and punching, pounding her desk for all she is worth which happens to be nothing. The boys take their weak unoriginal cue from her too and laugh loud in my face as I walk unafraid up to them.

She is blatantly swigging from a flask of brandy and throwing back some speed. 'You are the ugliest loser I've ever seen in my life, mate!' She laughs so much she is almost ill, then she belches violently and waves the shit on the stuck to pizza lids right under my face for good measure. They fall about pointing and laughing at me, tears of genuine aged-in-wood mockery cascading from their drugged and drunken eyes.

I lean into her young confused face and I say to her, 'You go and sit on your bottom on the linoleum in the corridor or I will throw you there.'

She quietens then says, 'You wouldn't do that!'

I say, 'Just try me. You've got six seconds to go and sit on the cold corridor or I will lift you up and drop you there!'

My eyes are like a grey and cold wolf; she realises I mean it. We lock glances for a minute then she runs quickly to the freezing cold hallway and sits straight away on the linoleum and slams the sliding door with a bang. Her lovers glare at me but they realise I am unafraid of anything now.

We begin to study the ancient foundations of metre, assonance and rhyme, and you've got to say they were not bad at it for kids so young but filled with potential. We worked hard at our new poems and after the first period of 60 minutes concluded I went out and asked her if she felt like re-joining the poetry class. She fumed and swore at me and slammed the sliding door on my runner.

But in the end she did relent and ran into the room and joined in the interested kids who were writing away for all they were worth, and she said to them, 'Where are we up to?' They worked so hard on their poetry and I felt pretty much vindicated.

Another lesson in humility I suppose and hopefully they all add up to a worthwhile career; it's just a fact that one can't be taught or even coerced to teach properly. There is no properly.

Tram Jack

Today is a frosty old October Monday and I viewed the telly last night upon Channel Two and the lugubrious weather gentleman informed me it was below freezing up at Mount Hotham, wherever that is it's not for me. I have always delighted in the rich skiing and so on in alpine holiday resorts, possibly I rejoice in their skiing more than they do, even with free artificial snowflakes but anyway it must have been chilly for the silly things.

I have manufactured fresh Vegemite sandwiches for my young son and inserted into a Garbage Bag (which was all I could find this morning to put his lunch in) and wished of course I'd had the foresight to buy him bananas last night for his nutrition and general well-being and we set off at 7am into the insanity of Boil Street to get him to high school on time. The conveyances on the highway today included a Panzer Division as well as mounted police ladies.

Greek fruitshop persons lie all over the road, anything for attention, and bread baskets split in two with tyre marks on them, people misjudging crucial distances between parked trees. I got him to his mother's terrace where he wanted to shower and he wanted to get himself to school himself, he said, anyway, so I drove back to my slum again and waited patiently in a tempest for the Sickening Road tram to Boil Street; the petrol my car uses is beyond anyone's income.

I stared at the usual suicidal travellers all packed in looking three quarters of the way to the grave, the tram chassis being the casket with wheels on. Not one single passenger smiled or looked a trifle pleasant, all were hideous and malformed with buboes and gnarled toes with a bell on their humped backs to warn of leprosy. I paid today for my ticket, which I usually don't do because it's not worth a cent to go to work these days, we all know that fact.

But I didn't feel like being hassled by a Haitian ticket examiner. I tried to think about what the first lesson was today until I became aware that it really meant getting off the tram. Forget the second lesson which is not getting upset by the gnomic travellers or atomic chipmunk driving the stupid tram.

Disagreeably the tram hiccuped and swayed oily and cranked about as trams invariably do when Germans insist on designing the things, and I stared put-out at dark fart marks imprinted indelibly in tram staff's cack-brown pants as they bent over children to frighten the devil out of them. Even the lady ticket checkers bore fart marks in their pants, the dirty objects of ridicule!

I felt a bit vague I have to tell you at the exhausting Monday Morning Conference where Brian was holding court, talking about the rise of unexpected male rape at the local Woolworths. He said it was mostly unexpected but sometimes it wasn't as unexpected as you might think. The Brunswick Police were keen to hear from any teachers who had been raped lately, either in their own homes by persons unknown or not necessarily pack raped in the duffel coat area of Woolworth.

Brian had slides of rapists projected on a screen that was dodgy and it was pretty hard to see any detail of any kind, apart from their buttocks or suitcases. The cleaners said they wouldn't mind being raped as they were so lonely being chaste and no one laughed because it isn't funny, well it is a bit I suppose, but you'd have to be in the right sort of mood.

Brian then led us into a question and answer segment that had to do with the ideological thread between the perceived notion of holiday and the actual poverty and boredom of it. He asked the staff where in the world they went for their break and they tried to remember just where that was. Fifteen staff confessed it was Coburg where the only thing that happened to them was to be drastically penalised by their local video outlet for excessive lateness in returning a DVD.

Brian coughed.

One teacher broke down before us all and sobbed as she told of her father feeling her up at the National Aquatic Centre, near the dolphin she said.

Another one said he stayed and home and boxed his father to death, but people couldn't tell if he was joking. Yet another said she'd developed whooping cough in her rental property out of indolence. She said she wished the holidays could be stopped. Her cocker spaniel had died of assumed whooping cough which has to do with wish fulfilment and is rare because cocker spaniels seldom copy their owners to Hell and beyond Coburg.

Of course and naturally the kids played vile air hockey deafeningly during the interminable conference while a few teachers went crook about The Mistress Of Urine still being overseas and still possessing the staff toilet keys and one lady teacher of maths said she had a bad back lately from all the hanging-on lately. She added that the loo at The Plaza was locked a lot lately and none of the pretentious cafes on the strip allowed non-customers to do wee or the other one unless they bought food there.

My first double Drama went swimmingly with the one armed boy writing elegantly, pausing only for a second to dab antiseptic gel on his stump because it gets so sore. I cried one day just seeing him do that. It was like the storm broke watching a poor boy like him do something so prosaic. I wanted to help him. I've always wanted to help anyone in trouble. That's why I became a teacher and I believe it's the sole reason for the profession.

We did sharing and the production of our review is now in rehearsal with the usual teething troubles actors face, such as trying to recall lines that are obscene or witty or written today, getting used to the new problem of acting with lighting, how baffling lighting can be if you're unused to its glare and the annoying popping of shattered bulbs all over the place.

We open next week I told the kids then tried out the brand new German toilet Brian had paid an arm and a leg for; it was for both or three sexes and boasted black bricks on the outside and black bricks on the inside, was twenty feet high and had hot and cold water and a little heater in it that warmed your bottom for you as you sat on it, but not too hot as to burn your anus. It had magazines on education in Israel that focused on decapitation of Arabs, and so on.

I was on my morning break and absolutely busting so I went out the back in the gruesome courtyard filled with hanged cats draped over rusty barbed wire gates and discarded teachers lying with their black tongues out all over the place and I beheld the mint-new German Loo and since it didn't need a key to defecate or urinate in, I went right in it at once.

It was so frightfully dark and sombre with its sophisticated-ness and so I carefully kicked my trousers off and hopped on it with eagerness and real need to jettison the muck I'd reluctantly nibbled over the last weekend in Coburg, which was the north wind mostly, mixed with footy frankfurts.

I groped for a light switch in order to view the bowl but a weak but insistent light came on without the bother of explanation of any technical kind and it emanated from the black grim bowl you sat on so the more you did something supposedly the brighter it became until the occupant fainted.

'Ten hours is your maximum use time!' demanded a voice chip based on Robinson Crusoe, how they archived his voice nobody knows, quite, but Brian lectured us that it was so it was, no doubt. Anything for authenticity.

I actually fell as I put my pants back on and went

right up in the air inside the dark of it. I really seriously hurt myself then, my nose a lot, my back even more. Then it wouldn't unlock no matter what I tried to get back to class.

I felt honestly the toilet had sort of kidnapped its occupant and that the maximum use time would come true. I beat and beat the padded door but open it refused to contemplate. I then had a fit and bit all the loo paper into tiny flutters all over the place of savage confinement. Someone came and let me out. From now on I use only the Plaza loo and just put up with the mile walk.

The groping for the invisible switch and the subsequent fall from grace which resulted in both a chipped tooth and a big dint in my ego resolved in me a certainty never to visit any sort of a toilet again in my lifetime endured in Sickening Road. I daydreamt that I was stung repeatedly and hurtfully and insistently by Egyptian mosquitoes as I emerged from a sarcophogus in Sickening Road; a kind of tabernacle or shrine somehow made by The Department Of Human Services.

My life became a voice chip and in separation with no human touch apart from me myself putting on my pants I became in love with all the voice chips that totally intoxicated and surrounded me, particularly at Boil Street where none of the staff could relate to me. I kind of hoped to be retrenched and in a way, a desultory way, looked kind of forward to retirement, but then again if you retire in Coburg there is nothing to do but die or eat Turkish.

I began to court a particular voice chip I'd first overheard on a guy's cell phone on the Coburg tram, and somehow it haunted me, visited me during double English lessons. I even heard it in the bath after work. It was the schizophrenic voice of some earlier me. It adored me madly and intensely and I joyously taught the children in an entirely revolutionary way because their ripostes no longer wounded me.

They could scarcely be ruder to me lately but I didn't hear them because my sweet voice chip had taken over and it sang to me as I corrected their essays and poems. I told my doctor at Coburg Medical Centre that I was in love with my voice chip and he told me I was insane and gave me some sleepers, not that he is supposed to do that kind of thing.

On my way home last night talking sweet nothings to my implant I looked up and realised I had never before been on so packed a tram. It was lurching and rattling and groaning and creaking and swaying stuffed full of smelly men and women who hadn't laughed since they came through their mother's womb in The Old Country. It was soaked with the infection called Loneliness Of The Spirit.

Not one body on it wished in any real or abstract way to be on it. The black bodies of Greek ladies swathed in a perpetual sadness since their pumpkin-grower-husband dropped dead getting on a similarly overcrowded tram, leaving their horrid walking cane jammed in the runningboard as a stroke overcame them, thank Christ, then they didn't have to live in

Coburg another day, and went back to Athens at once, to play cards and eat honey cakes.

Two strange tram staff slammed the doors shut with mechanical aid so the sound it made, the tram, was like two palms applauding inside some vast vacuum. The driver made an announcement in a blurry inaudible way that they always do that it was not going to pull up ever again.

People screamed and shrieked; some clapped in approval in the sure knowledge they would die on the awful thing, much better than eating with relatives you need to bury, far happier a prospect for sure than living with a lady who detests you and switches on the telly whenever you are by, in order to mask your bullshit. So many wives in Coburg resort to this ruse just to bear their uninteresting husbands who could not converse with a carrot-grater.

It was a tram jack, the first one ever in the complete history of transport in our country. The tram went flat out to the depot in Essendon without ever stopping, even though immigrants wept in the cramped step wells and tipped over deliberately their shopping trolleys stuffed to the gunwales with cantaloupes and frozen pies and imitation food from the Old Country baked in Coburg. At the depot there were ambulances available to deal with the exhausted poor pilgrims who'd been driven at sensational speed 60 kilometres out of their area in under five minutes, an Olympic record if ever there were one.

I did a thing I don't ever do any more as a rule, and that is I went up the pub and fought my way through to the sticky bar top and hoarsely ordered a pint of V.B. and I smoked in the fogginess and rudeness and tried to ignore fourteen-year-old ladies with hardly anything on who sipped scotches and in my imagination winked at me. I drank for hours and ended up discussing the mystery of the Australian Zodiac with the cleaner, a police informant and former Geography teacher at Glenroy High School.

I took home two bottles of plonk and sat up the yard in pouring rain drinking each until they were out then I fried some off steak in the pan and read my gas bill disconnection account for an hour at my kitchen table, continuing smoking and drinking until the television set blew right up. Good one, I thought. Good one again.

I slept in pre natal position for drunkards and dreamt I was young again. In the morning I put on the telly and there was a bulletin on Channel Ten about the tram nap but I didn't really recognise anyone on board. My son came over and we played tennis all morning on this new asphalt court I found a week ago in Essendon that is never locked. In the boot were two reasonably decent balls and I got all my first serves in, but my son won the first set six to none. We shook hands at the net, as per normal.

I read on the way to work about the notorious tram highjacker and was crushed to learn he was experiencing clinical depression coupled with high anxiety attacks that he rinsed partly away with a near-lethal combination of multi-B vitamin capsules and dreadfully expensive anti-depressive compounds found in gibbons. Strange to relate the sufferer doesn't require any prescription for any of these drugs and as long as there's money in your pants you just venture into any pharmacy and look terrible and through the use of pantomime they give it to you without a qualm. I read that the tram thief was taken to Coburg Police Station and charged with tram stealing. There was scarce mention of forcing passengers to gnaw a sausage at his own home. The media seems to ignore these titbits somewhat.

It is now Tuesday and Brian collapsed at our Tuesday conference, complaining of gas before he expired right on the old belt-driven photocopier – he certainly didn't look too good – nor did his reproduction as it whisked out of a side vent and then due to some mistake or other made by an earlier user of the photocopier hundreds of fairly good quality photocopies flew out of our poor old principal looking blue around the gills.

Some of us took him on the school stretcher to the staff sick bay at the rear of the chapel and although he was pretty trembly they put a blanket or two over him until he recovered, which was right on the last bell at 4pm when the hall shuts. Brian was thought to need a holiday fairly soon, like all of us. He was real bad just before knock-off-time and The Mistress Of Urine's personal assistant slid him two Panadol.

I was going through all the invites in my filthy plywood pigeonhole and found one that requested the pleasure of my company at Choir. I had nothing to do at 5pm so I hung around the chapel after Brian drove home in his wind-powered Saab and waved cheerfully at me as he hammered into choked Sickening Road and immediately got himself multi-tailgated by billions of dangerous cars and big trucks with Viking horns on.

It was a homeless group in our church who sang beautifully, almost divinely you'd have to think if you were luckily in their midst. They were dressed in their native rags and the words to their hymns were written on the bright or dull stripes of collapsed mattresses held up by depressed assistants on medication. It was an inspiring sight to say the least; especially when they sang 'Abide With Me' so soothingly even the sparrows sighed and ceased nibbling.

After Choir was Boxing and the very same hymn-mattress was exploited in a new way, and that was to act as an impromptu boxing-ring that supported the stressed-out combatants as they shaped up to each other and dodged and feinted and beat each other up in a no-mucking-about kind of a way. The work experience kid filmed each bloodthirsty round until he ran out of film. The kids' parents either cheered or swore or kicked one another rather a lot.

Tuning in to Only Nature was my Teacher's Breakthrough

Some days I don't want to go in and yet others I can't really wait for the kids to dawdle in to me, with agape mouths, disinterested eyes, hungry tummies and chronic fatigue syndrome and this is the worst of all debilitations to demoralise the landscape of my not-asked-for birth. I'm not saying here I didn't request birth in my mother's womb, that was restful, it was laid-back I remember, with my own little library stocked with a decent free supply of heavenly prose to take a geek at.

The fact is it's again raining, again inclement and some days I just want to dawdle as the kids dawdle, although it isn't so good an idea to dawdle during pelting rain. I have a ghastly premonition I shall die of pneumonia; we'll just have to wait and see whether pneumonia has any premonition of murdering me by the fantastic withdrawal of breath.

Some days in rainy mid-September when my memoir was completed by hailstones that typeset the darting message of my educational emotions that I really do adore to teach but am tired of the ministry of Gloom coming down on me for daring to be the Daniel who walks with thongs on into the lion's den but I do it just like he did because getting through to somebody, anybody, is such a turn-on. You get higher than the original audience who listened to Aesop when he taught at Preston Tech.

When I get home a lady who bought a painting from me a while ago has shouted me my rental property being mown by a professional gardener and he's already been so I can get in. It was six-foot high round the back last night because I sat out there getting into the white wine and cigarettes and couldn't see the back of the house. I checked the back and he'd done the back. I felt an absurd swelling up of rental pride because I know I'll never own anything but the love of my son.

I made a mental note to buy a rubbish bin because the place is filthy in the extreme use of that word. I used an old Dickies beach towel to rinse down the cooking area then dried same with two *Ages*. I rinsed the Willow pattern dinner dishes and got ready for Lou to come. He had a good day at school he said and he reclined in his special reclining chair and put his great big flat feet on the electric heater; his eyes are the most beautiful things I've ever looked into the both of.

'What's for dinner, Dad?' he sang out just then, after he'd put on Channel Ten which is the only station we watch. We view it from six till ten then fall asleep. If it's not too freezing outside we sometimes have a boot of the ball in the park over from the slum although the council have wisely put a dogshit bag collector object in it to collect all the fresh dogshit bags and you have to watch out or you could be castrated by the thing.

'Good torp, Dad!,' he cries triumphantly as I pull up a beauty, right to his slim chest that is so strong and impressive. He's turning into a man right in front of baggy-eyed me of sixty-odd. I boot the footy with all my might and it's a good punt kick that I manage to get through the chains of the swings and slides to him. We often do that just to play together for the fun. It's a great impulse to sing out and escape teaching.

We have dumplings at a dumpling shop in the strip with hundreds of other Barrys and Louis doing the same because dumplings are popular after the liquification of The World Trade Centre. Or at least it seems they are – isn't that when they came in? Stupidly I tip loads of brownish vinegar over a bowl of lovely fresh hot dumplings to muck them up. I thought they were soy in those idiotic little tipper things.

'Wrecked, thanks a lot!,' declares my aghast son. I tip soy on next and he munches several and gives me the timeless thumbs-up. 'Not as good as last time we had dumplings, Dad,' he shrugs and I look up and notice a fifty-stone couple trying to sit. Why do persons want to die, I think, then we pay and walk back home across hectic Boil Street where foreigners stand there looking as lost as we are.

He sits up late to enjoy the footy and the footy gossip and I rinse my dentures and then check just how ugly I am before hitting the sack. I don't look too bad for an old bloke and see my face as sweet which it mostly is. The black eye bags are more intense so that I look like Fatty Arbuckle who I am in fact. I wash my hay-fever eyes and sloosh my mouth out with council swamp water from the tap in the clogged hand basin. Shall I ever make love again or repair to the grave?

The night is kind to me and thoughtful and I drift into unconsciousness almost on cue after a good day's teaching and feeling relieved my son is stopping over. He has a good room of his own and likes to listen to classical music before sleep kicks in, his long legs so perfect and straight for a brilliant athlete like him, thank providence.

The entire weekend hay fever and each entire hour of each entire episode saw your writer not merely sneeze an inordinate amount thus piling up Mount Everest heaps of saturated Kleenex tissues into each I blew my whole life and all the pain and longing in it.

I have never sneezed so much in all my life in fact. I sneezed and swore into my own crumpled blanket thus creating sudden dams and lakes composed of hurtful compounds of transparent mucus that plagued me all of the night I devoted each billowing into either the back of my hand or anything I could wheeze and sputter into. My back it ached and my throat all bulged and extremely enlarged and boiled-up from the virus.

I got up and continued coughing and spluttering all over my gas accounts that I was inserting into waterlogged envelopes with mucus stamps snorted on; imagine trying to be a good secretary to a good public servant with a chronic hay fever attack!

My underpants wet through from some sort of preposterous senility. My hair all wet and damp from the onset of stupidity syndrome and my athletic chest all heaving and concave from a trillion blows of my poor old nose!

It never ended, the night just would not ever conclude and it's amusing and no it isn't because when you're quite alone and sick, even with side-splitting hay fever which is the vaudeville of all respiratory conditions you fail to detect the hilarious side of it because you are just about dead from it.

I awoke yesterday to death by virus of the nose which was like a billion knitting needles sawing right through my gastric construction; the pain manifest just putting damp shirt back on that you've blown muck into all night long in perfect and blind delirium, my whole bedroom mucus.

I sat at 4am in the kitchen striving to relax with the pneumonia fact of no breath for breath-fast.

I tried to feebly and most pathetically spoon into me a dreary bowl of inedible Cheerios with a splash of tetanus milk but my jaw was so enlarged and my gums so swollen and my swallowing apparatus so bad I just couldn't sip it. I went out the overgrown backyard and with nothing on I got through next-door's shattered fence and thieved some fresh lemons.

I painstakingly hand ruptured six bosom-looking squat lemons from next door's tree and waited six years for the kettle to boil; I then tried hard to plonk a forkful of incredibly difficult honey into my teacup but the honey was so tough it wouldn't fold. I sat in my rental kitchen naked without a hope.

Men are dogs and it's certainly true of barky me that I can't look after my body that good; not that it ever goes crook: in fact my body is like my ancestor's ones it just keeps going. I blew my swollen nose more and more only adding to the heap of awful loo paper on my tabletop.I blew my nose half hoping it would just come right off my poor red face. I drove the car to the pharmacy but it was shut even though they say they are open.

I hammered down ugly Sickening Road until I found a chemist shop that was trading. I would gladly have put a brick through a window of one to get hay fever capsules to give me drugged relief. I purchased a pack of eight tablets and the old girl there was put-out that I'd asked for a cup of water and really couldn't see why she should give it to me. I just gulped the tabs down with the H_2O.

I drove home badly half expecting two hay fever cops to pull me over in a wall of germs.

After two more hours of sneezing and choking I felt better, maybe it's just all the pollen lately, I don't know why I was so bad. My son Louis and I had a hit of the tennis ball at the Fitzroy Tennis Club and although I was wheezy and whistly I hit a few good ones; not like him who hit only very good ones. He is balletic, Lou.

Last Saturday he played for Clifton Hill against their mortal enemy Ivanhoe. I put the early morning wake-up call on for 6am but when it went off it didn't make any ring noise, typical of Optus.

Though both chaps studied the Melways Street Directory just like monks taking a look-see at Genesis, we couldn't work out where the Ivanhoe Tennis Club was. We got in the car and went looking, with Lou holding the map. I found two incorrect courts in The Boulevarde that only led to another Boulevarde. We found it in the end but the second we got there this Chinese lady with an aggressive air said our club would have to suffer a walkover because 'one of the fathers' was late meaning me. I struggled to placate the stupid bitch but she sort of said it would be okay to play them as if she herself owned the idiotic club that hasn't got a single Koori in it, only Chinese.

The game went for four years. I have never been so sick of anything in my life as that game. My son played well with his new partner Sam who is slim and nimble just like Lou is. They laughed and joked on the instant, not like the Lutherans that took two hours to fire up the barbecue and sting me two fifty a snag. He played well and had the enjoyment of good young company so was happy in the young sunshine. I marvelled to myself at his effortlessness and sheerest agility all over the court that day. He went home to stay with his mother who had just got back from a school camp and I went to my dump to get asthma, bronchitis and drop dead.

After dropping my son to school and risking my hide trying to pull in for a second so he can actually undo the door and get out with his bag and all the hateful heathen parents tailgate me so they can screw another parent in a motel for forty-five dollars and then swot up on human rights as reported in the conservative press the day starts always bad or tense is much closer to the actual sensation because you become tense when you relax in the company of your betters.

They have better wives as you have none; they drive better because they're not poor; they smile better because they boast teeth whereas you just gulp at things. They set the table for supper then whip the assistants out in the barn for dishing up food joylessly; you live mostly with no one so you chew Coles steak brimful of gristle and heavenly thick fat on the floor by Channel Ten.

I drive home at eight thirty and grab an instant black coffee and take a look at the paper which is always demoralising, including stories that denude you and deprave you and completely take all your go out of you with their take on mayhem all around you, blown up large to make you feel much worse that what you were when for some un-asked for reason you woke.

On my way to the first lesson is the eternal conundrum of eternal beauty and just how overwhelming elegance is and how elusive it is and how prosaic it often is and how it can't be taught in any way, shape or formlessness or even describe how startling this or that spectacularly lit-up young face is, this dreamy visage coming down the street with moronic parents talking about what they are having for dinner in 2050.

The incredibly innate face carved out of wonder

is young kids. It doesn't matter much if they have inquiring minds or Leonardo minds or are brain-dead like their parents are; you can really tell if their parents are possessed of any grey matter by the way they look. Parents tend to fall to type and thus you can see in a second if they can read, forge cheques or win Power Ball midweek.

I know life is briefer than my gloom and I am mindful of my overbearing crypt that whispers Sylvia Plath's marvellous sentences to me in my whirling crazy bed that won't ever take a break from thinking. Sometimes my favourite times I am right in it, the education pleasure gene and giving it out holus bolus to grateful children who realise learning's the drug they need to hit.

There is a friendly muse in the musing air, the air is conditioned to relaxation which is English's best friend and the desks of awful Boil Street are still for once and not being scuffed or booted for once and their exercise books are filling themselves up with marvellous sentences that defy analysis of how they got there because the whole double English class was nothing but a groove from start to finish and because the happy hardworking kids had a ball they didn't know what to do with you in the room with them so they clapped you.

The approbation of fairies!

When teaching is like this you never want to quit and the lesson stays with you like a sweet reminder that you are here not for you but the love of others, no matter how destructive or repulsive they happen to be. It's a war-field, a battle-board with a chalk chap out the front who offers literature of excrement to them unless it's new and exactly how they see life as both sewer-pit and the elysium.

You have entertained very tiring and very tired kids for eighty minutes of excitement mixed with peace; you have enchanted them and they have composed essays worth remembering and not just for the record. Only yesterday they had you by the short and curlies and boo'd you as you came in to get yours. Now they are in a state of grace and are writing better than you can, not that that's so great. You got them thinking! Good on you!

One loathsome acne boy called Bobby lives only by anaemically kissing his pneumatic-breasted buck-toothed girlfriend who swears like a trooper. If she isn't in class he won't work, learn or think. He just dives deeper down into his filthy opshop vinyl parachute jump-suit with the big silver gaffer tape patches velcro'd onto its bottom which is where his head is at the minute. He is so entrenched within his own appalling filthy garment, particularly the bottom of it, the pants that when I say to him 'Good morning somewhere in there,' he says 'Get fucked', to which he adds the postscript, 'I'm not doin' this shit!' I do wish he and I would stop swearing.

The kids are mucking around and only Simon can prise a syllable out of them because he knows them and has mastery over them and is their shepherd. He will see them get a job and if they stick with Simon home is a distinct possibility and I am in dumbfound awe of Simon.

You walk through the walls of Coburg Market an hour after your miracle is over. The usual grotesques are screaming at you to purchase poisoned sausages; the usual ghostly cauliflower vendors are casting crumpled stalks at you in their determined effort to pay their meaningless mortgages. I go home and put Channel Ten on.

One particular Friday after work for the first time in forty-one years of being there I was invited to drinks in the chapel, and to my own surprise said affirmative rather than negative. I hardly ever socialise and sort of prefer to bump into people in the street with whom I have no rapport. I sometimes don't admire the human race and shy away from practising Zombies because they can be just so mean, abrasive, unhelpful and can have your guts for garters as some lady sang somewhere in a music hall.

All our teachers work hard – you only have to ask them – and it is a given that trying to educate tough kids likje them can be a touchy-feely enterprise and not only are the pupils difficult but they are capable of intense meanness that can not only sting but completely deflate your already saggy spirits.

Most of the teachers don't have hay fever and so can see what they are chalking on the rotating blackboard, or even see crystal-clear when they peer into their state of the art computers. Most of the classes are on-line including mind reading. They prefer high technical teaching that comes complete with sighing and looking cool and postmodern, whatever that is I'm no good at it. I am an original Sloth.

The teachers are obsessed with looking detached where I am really as detached as The Dead. I have never ever grown up and still say, without self-consciousness, 'Thanks a lot', and 'Please' in my daily rounds. I even thank the police for insulting me when they see my front number plate has finally come right off the front end.

I go to unconsciousness in my despair and singlet and go to work the same way, depending on what sort of daily or hourly weather it is on the day, I might slide a hotter top on to prohibit pneumonia because I don't want to die of it.

The young teachers probably live with their young parents to save on paying rent; they probably gnaw multi vitamin capsules at the breakfast table in a hurried sort of way and gobble toast and gargle correct save the rainforest coffee beans then their policeman parents drive them to the railway stop.

It is four in the afternoon and Brian Epstein has invited the Year Ten kids to perform an obscene concert at ear-canal exploding high definition, they are called 'The No-Goods' and I have to sit right down the front next to sixteen bisexual maths ladies. The light is blinding me and Brian himself is up there in the rigging frigging round with the lights.

You cannot hear a single thing anyone is trying to tell you.

The noise is beyond crediting or editing. The young teachers have been getting stuck into booze of all kinds and the mathematics ladies are going the grope in their black leather jackets and deliberately fragmented fishnet stockings. Everybody is dancing but me and screaming 'Go for it!'

Other teachers from local schools drop over and the booze is really flowing by now, with cask red proving very popular with Koori maths teachers who have just got back from a city rally over Israel's unlawful occupation of Palestine. I didn't know it was unlawful.

The Pure Horror of Collaboration

This day is Hell pure and not simple as I should have assumed rightly or wrongly Purgatory's charm is that one can never be certain what the next awful moment shall be and that its variance is crucial to its frisson. Today everything I have striven for is shattered through the worst thing in any world and that is collaboration.

Ms Tina Dull has been chosen by Arts Mentone to augment the tiny written scenes the kids have brilliantly or reluctantly cobbled together with me at the ragged helm; she is so sure of her talent but I have witnessed her interpretation of nightmares before in live theatre that was stillborn the moment it started. Her style of theatre is truth and as we most of us realise there isn't any.

She is tall and angular and rides her former partner's unicycle to work with a steely look that goes with the arrogant look of the bike itself. She listens to Brian our principal with the world-weary artifice of all drongos. She is now working on the crucial editing of the kid's hand-written scene is the chapel and it is thought the script is going well although no one as usual knows a single thing, not about life or writing or breathing.

As I head in the leafy and geranium'd gate I see Brian frigging round in the school portable where he wishes he were teaching Latin, not that he can read it or speak it, but apparently he once had a mother who used to be Italian and she said she could read it, so there may be a connection to Latin no matter how tenuous.

Brian Epstein called me in and so I went in and excitedly said 'Ms Dull is now in, indeed she has been recently detected going in the chapel in order to have a first read-through of the review. She has a natural sense of authority do not you find? It's in her gait mostly, although everything about her is authoritative. Why don't you go over to the chapel and give her a hand to work on the kid's script?'

So I hightailed it over there thinking it will be enjoyable to hear the scenes read aloud, discussed. I opened up the frigid chapel door which felt rather like pulling Christ's head off his shoulders. It had an unholy feeling, although I mean to say why would it – isn't a chapel a perfectly natural place to work with charity and kindness?

The very sorry second I pulled up inside she was the witch from Sickening Road you'd never want to collide with. She had the kids silent and seated at her feet like the Beatles lyric from Lady Madonna. I had never ever seen them silent and was just so acquainted with their action, mayhem and tearing around being rude 24/7; yet here they simply were, contained as a sore foot.

They even looked intelligent as though she had given them a spray of intellect. She was so untired-looking and pure against her silent charges who were clearly frightened of her, physically and mentally. The chapel even had its heating on because she had clearly nutted out just how it came on. The gas was scared of her of course and came on of its own volition.

The kids I hardly recognised yet I had taught them for years ever since their junkie mothers bore them in community hospices as crummy as our old school hall. They seemed to bear different expressions from the snarly ones of yore; they were at some sort of baffling peace that she had inspired them to go into. Maybe she is a decent teacher I thought as I skidded to a halt before her icy statuesqueness.

She held her witch finger over her harsh mouth as though to say to me 'Shush thanks!' I did have a bit of a big lump in the rear of my throat, that invariably occurs whenever I'm being bullied, as in now as she puts the strictures on me not to speak or move lest I show perfect disrespect to one of my legion of betters. But there is nobody greater than she of the great stillnesses.

There are twenty kids altogether; gawking straight into my old blue eyes so I look like Frank Sinatra poached. They have never looked intent before and yet she has them intent and ramroad-straight before her thraldom. She stands at her full and imperial height which is exactly sixteen feet tall, give or take a searing look she has learnt at witch's camp for community theatre workshops organised by the Devil.

She is of course black as the ace of spades including black lipstick and slightly now she grates and grinds her pulverising eye teeth as she takes me in, a reprobate. There is sheer stillness in the awful air of the 1834 chapel where it is rumoured Mathew Flinders moored his rowboat after he discovered Melbourne. The kids aren't moving but instead stare at me like that horror film I saw in 1964 *The Children Of The Damned* where their demonic eyes go all pale and deadly serious when they intend to kill someone, anyone will do in their village.

She speaks in that dead real voice of hers laced with arsenic and old hate of lesser artists like me who deigned to interrupt her lesson in script editing. Those terrifying warts tremble bunion-wise all over the bridge of her two-yard nose that leads like lunacy to her bucky teeth then the mean throat does the rest to you. You drop dead when she speaks, as was foretold in The Book Of The Dead written by a long dead bureaucrat who laboured for the Education Department.

'I thought that we were meeting Friday yet you turn up on a Thursday.' That is all she has to tell me to put me in my place which is nowhere. She almost laughs at my embarrassment, my predicament of losing face in front of the kids I have taught for so long and completely against their wishes. I need to dig a hole then get right in it.

I stammer, 'Brian told me to pop in the chapel so we could edit the writing together; I thought that you'd like that because two heads are much better than one –

are they not?' I became a hesitant idiot trying to justify my chapel'd presence. She indicated the exit sign on the door.

I walked back upstairs again to my dorm room and helped a newborn child do some nursery rhymes with a crayon. He ended up sitting on my cold leg and I drew funny pictures for it, whatever sex it was. 'Gee that's a funny drawing.' The child laughed but I wept. She had broken me, that bitch from community theatre, and I just couldn't cease caterwauling; not that the baby on my leg cared. It did not because it knew I loved it for merely being alive within the meaning of public education.

A funny thing happened after that on my luncheon break at 1pm when in Sickening Road I tripped right over a hundred buck note that some guy or chick had dropped. I put it up to my good eye and assumed it was a photocopy from work because often a staffer photocopied his pay for something positive to do other than shoot up.

I went into a fashionable gambling venue next door to our hall and took it all in. Thousands of idiots doing their dole using unwinnable pokies and chainsmoking lung droppings and sucking on wine at only one in the day. Idiot mothers losing their savings on two-cent gaming machines and contented to do so, I have to say. The airconditioning smelled of burnt pork.

Vietnamese servants serving burnt pig to ocker pigs who had it made; prostitutes throwing back the heroin in plain sight as they got their egos aligned with Mars.

I ordered a steak but when it came I ran out the back and vomited over a bouncer who didn't mind, not in the slightest. I hadn't had a thing of breakfast except my heart condition tabs and washed those down with a weak tea. But the atmospherics of that tavern connected with my human despair at modern existence so I barfed.

I hate vomiting, it is a thing I don't do as a rule in life, our little go at life, but the way she put me down, so much she did and with such a mix of imperiousness and justification made me crook in the tummy, which is where all truth be told. Later on she swept into my own dorm room and she didn't apologise in any expected way at all, which felt odd, but she looked at me like a rodent about to eat a pie, or something like that. I felt hated by her on her first day or maybe she'd been there a lifetime, conjured by the devil out of the chapel keyboard.

I was working with a child on her literacy and that kid was sitting on my knee, cold knee since one of them hadn't got the heating going as per usual but the new drama coordinator looked askance at me as if I were a bit of nothing that required sweeping aside, and I hated I must say the way she kept on rubbing her sage jaw with the shivering but not minding the shivering back of her witch's hand as she gawked hard at me to put me right off, which is evil's aim every day we live under it.

'You must learn to knock in my workshop before you just barge in in future,' she drawled and the child on my knee ran off so I was quite alone with the frightful thing. She sighed hard as she leant on my writing which was a sonnet I was composing to a deteriorating girlfriend who told me sex was an ego trip and she's a grandmother.

'I only came to you because Brian asked me to work with you; that was the only real reason I came to you and I have to say I was shocked by your rudeness to me. You waved your great arm at me and dismissed me like I was your serf.' She gave a bad breath smile and earbashed me about winning the children's confidence. To my astonishment the cinematographer came in with her and started filming her new put-down on me for the record. It was a thing I couldn't believe that he could possibly do.

'I'm just filming you for the record,' he said, and I hated him more than her if that's possible. In that moment of great and instant distress I hated him. She and he seemed to be an item. Maybe she was pregnant to him, the cinematographer. Maybe not because I couldn't imagine any man loving her, holding her in bed, it would have to be choreographed and approved by her, the motif would be her motif, her teeth were her motif.

The cinematographer was too scared to ask for his weekly payment to be the school voyeur. He was always thirsty and hopelessly hungry without a buck in his pants to purchase food to keep the crank-handle going on his movie camera. I took him out to a trendy breakfast once in June when it was down to five below on the streets of North Pole Brunswick when junkies lay beneath semi-trailers to try and keep warm.

I asked him at the crap coffee shop up the road from work why he didn't put in an invoice for his labours but he said there was no rush. Well yes there was because everyone else was paying for his food. One day he literally fainted for want of sustenance next to our photocopier; anyway his camera got seriously dinted when he fell on his face. I shouted him a plate of hot scones and jam and clotted cream. 'I didn't possibly deserve this,' he mock-protested with a gob full of cream. 'Eat up,' I said from somewhere deep in my fatherhood.

Now I am working with Umberto the Italian lad, the one who when I first encountered him commenced to eat a pound of stick glue and then another pound of the stuff as well as rubbing the substance greasily round his be-whiskered jowls like a fully grown walrus might do with an entree of fish far out at sea.

'Where have you been!' he screamed delightedly at my form as tried hard to fit into the door. 'Well, Umberto,' I said with a smile as he sat and broke the chair, 'I have been working with other kids.'

'I don't like it when you do that!' he shrieked and head banged the impenetrable desk till it fell apart at once. 'We all must try to get on, Daniel, in this world that can be so at odds with our daily expectations.' 'You suck!' he hissed hard as hard and I examined all the slag on the remnants of a once good desk that was by now in bits on the filthy floor.

He wrote well and acted out the street dialogue in a witty way because his father runs the big fruitshop over from work, and Umberto can perfectly take off various purchasers of pineapples and buyers of bananas and acquirers of coconuts. He's a mimic, Umberto, with incredible fat on him and pimples all up his neck and big back, but he's a writer, no doubt.

He works hard on dialogue and acts it out well so I can see and hear the people he's doing. He hugs me hard, forgets my name and I his, then we part and I go and join in the meeting after school. The talk is on the prevalence of youth suicide and I am glad that Umberto is happy and going to Italy with his honest and hardworking parents. Everyone deserves a break.

For a funny but inexplicable reason all the next day went like Swiss clockwork except all the clocks are made in Sickening Road and the kids ticked alongside the clocks of life that tick away the mystery of time passing; the most infuriating aspect in life is the problem of where the seconds have all gone and where time has once problematically existed and yet nothing whatsoever remains of it, no matter where you happen to peep. Pupils today are existing in infinitesimal seconds of the alphabet designed by themselves.

Today is now and now is Preps or Preparatory Pupils Of Boil Street and Brian Epstein has spotted me skulking off in the so friendly dark after work last night and told me Preps are starting the following day and he wants me to be their Art and English Teacher.

I said okay without bothersome thought and just went home like normal and had my single supper on the vinyl right on the dot of seven when I always view the evening news bulletin on The ABC.

I am awaiting the Peps in my sepulchral room where I may as well be composing my Last Will And Testament. I am looking at the things of use before the winking grave. Pencils and sharpeners and old crumpled exercise books filled with swear words and compass holes all through them. The little and useless desks the kids engrave with hate and the suffocating truanting dust motes that glide into children's ears in order to read distraction to them if they are the slightest fraction artistic and some of them are but mostly their parents are not.

I can easily detect the atonal notes of the braying donkey parents depositing their infants on our school doorstep, the usual curses and sharp notes of personal abuse with threats of not bothering to come home that night, accompanied by children hoping and praying that threat is genuine. Kids who don't just live on the street but eat it wholesale, brick by brick and sugar-hit by sugar-hit. The parents have nothing to do all the day and sleep separately each night because that is hurtful to one of them who still hangs out for the other one of them. Greenies.

Seven spoilt-rotten four-year-old children are in my care as we go to press. They hate being seated next to each other and they hate everything in life, particularly Mr Dickins, me. I ask them how they are going and they just roll their large doll-like opticals in purest sarcasm. 'Not a bad day today?' I ask them but one of them says he had no idea he would have to be taught by anyone as old.

I sharpen pencils and suddenly realise that every single black lead writing pencil has my name on it connected to a swear word. I hand out butcher's paper upon which to write or draw or swear. One little girl, a brat who is deliberately lactose-intolerant, says with a screwed-up nose that has black and dark green mucus coming in and out of it, 'I hate you and I hate cheap butcher's paper. It is awful to the touch exactly as you are awful to the eye. I wish you death!'

I handed out the butcher's paper anyway and sipped some perfectly dreadful coffee that saves a rain forest with every slurp. It was very cold in my dorm room and the arseholes were shivering a fair bit so I went and pinched another teacher's heater – she doesn't seem to mind because she's always screaming to keep her body warm. It felt great to take it.

I got right down on my old arthritic knobbly knees with cheap bandaids over each and frigged round trying hard to patch the heater into the power-board with mouse dags all through it and all squashy stuff on the frayed extension lead. You quite feel like patching the cord into your old cold bum after a winter here.

The kids were all biting each other in front of me and gouging each other's eyes out with tremendous satisfaction; I didn't of course know their little Prep names so I went over two of them who were trying to kill one another with a length of exhaust flange, with a pool of gore on the floor and one of them braining the other of them with all of his force, repeatedly striking him with the off-cut of hard metal exhaust flange he's sheared off the faulty air-conditioner.

I stood over their biting writhing atheletic four-year-old brawling bodies and said, to my own stupefaction, 'Alastair I don't believe you ought to be braining Moses with that jagged length of metal that way you are. I don't think Moses is enjoying that.' To which Moses, all covered with blood said underneath the triumphant Alastair, 'How do you know what I like?' Fair point.

I sent them both off to the loo but naturally it was all padlocked since she was still overseas or was that the back-up teacher? One revolting cherub soiled itself precisely like an old drunkard in William Street and the other five of the things read Danish porn until I came back in the room. I rather felt like crying in sympathy with them.

By and by I hand the paper out and commence to draw with them and write poetry, too, but within a minute the novelty wears off and they need to hit and harm again; they know much better than to bite Mr Dickins as he would most definitely bite them back. One of them traces his revolting fingers into the mortar grooves that once housed a missing double-brick and he says to me like this in his obscene Greenie-worthy-voice, 'Where's the brick?' I don't recognise him.

They have no concentration and kick the chairs and boot their Chiko Rolls across the desks and gnaw each other. I offer them with kindness a tub of repellent coloured pencils and tell them they were made by blind people in Africa however that doesn't cut it.

I ask them if they'd like to go into teaching and they tell me to go and drop dead immediately if not sooner. I persevere until 11am and they then go off to morning play.

I go for my break and once again munch a rotten Vietnamese salad roll on my seat in Sickening Road; the flaky crumbs go everywhere and I keep on shaking my opshop jumper all the time to try and get rid of them-hopeless task! The sun is weaker than The Labor Party.

All round me are cashed-up lesbian cyclists who pay more than I earn per week as a teacher on Latin private lessons given by another one of them. Women of superb ugliness pushing bikes with hideous babies whose gaping expressions are just deposits for jam that's all in their hair. Bookshops run by monsters who hate the bookloving public. One of my friends on Sickening Road is Ken Anderson who used to run a cheap secondhand bookshop. We used to have coffees together until he sold up.

One rainy day he showed me how tough it was to try and run a reasonable cheap secondhand bookshop that is welcoming to every sort of passing nutter. 'Take a look at what this junkie did to my book on the first floor.' He showed me a Harold Robbins book which I think was called *The Carpet Baggers*. In it was a great big turd that the junkie had left in it by way of insult or free commentary.

'Gee, Ken,' I sympathised as I unfolded its incredible foulness that made my eyes water. 'That's so low a thing to do in such a friendly shop like yours.' He shrugged and smiled and gulped a fair bit at me and told me it was commonplace and to be expected these days now Harold Robbins isn't getting the reviews he once got. My turn to shrug and to smile. What a world we live in!

Now my morning break is over I front the Preps again because Brian reckons I have a genuine rapport with the little things. One girl tells me she hates me but needs to urinate so I tell her to go and do wee in the front bushes, which she does but accidentally urinates on her high fashion sandals. She comes back and tells me I'm uninteresting.

I hand out the butcher's paper again and several of the things have a seizure. Some of them do some work and we practise our old friend the alphabet in Texta. We write such words as curette or bowel cancer then pack up. One little girl writes a poem she plagiarised from Dylan Thomas but actually it's not bad and she has amended it to make it her own. When I congratulate her she slags all over my friendly face and I have to go to the bubblers and rinse her abuse of me off with foul public water.

Officeworks have offered to publish the Preps' fiction so maybe tomorrow they shall be a little more circumspect with their cutting remarks and even spit a little less.

We have been invaded by meanness. It is in the culture and in the public drinking water, unfortunately. Kindness is old-fashioned and abuse is modern.

During lunch I have to give a spoken report on how it went with the Preps, although that is hard to do since none of the staff are listening to a single word I say. They are emailing reports to each other whilst I give my report.

You lie because that is the only way to be believed.

I say the Preps are imaginative and come at things in an entirely new way and the staff clap me with spontaneous tears of piety in their eyes that have seen it all, known it all, as in *The Four Quartets* by T.S. Eliot.

All of a sudden I am tired and just sit on the old shapeless couch in the middle of the awful hall and watch the expertise of the young teachers run through its inspiring paces; the big boobed buck-toothed girlfriend of the illiterate boy who retreats, poor thing indeed, into the rear of his opshop silver gaffa taped parachute that he wears, sleeps in. She goes the pash on him and I am pleased because that is much better for him than a pass in Year Ten English. Well, not really!

The kids won't ever get a job after here; I know that much. Take a look at them throwing coffee pots at one another, operating the photocopier without anything in it to make a copy of, doing stuff that doesn't ever fit, make any sense, throw scraps of future unemployment at each other. Kick the Shorter Oxford Dictionary across a crowded room. Bray at thinking and guffaw at work, the most ridiculous thing. The cleaners come in at five and use a giant robotic vacuum cleaner to suck up all the waste. It's late and I'm in the public car park of Barkly Square Shopping Centre. Thank God no one has knocked off my Honda yet. I buy some tomatoes and motor home through the swearing.

It takes an hour some nights to go three miles to my hovel due to traffic. I pull up feeling too old to do it any more, you know, teach at 62 and check my letterbox for mail devoured by insatiable North Coburg snails.

I light a candle to save my soul in the bathroom and pray to Jesus Christ the Rheem Hot Water Service comes on in a new way: to whit it works! I kick off the human underpants of a man and check my grizzly face in the bathroom mirror. I put the red towel the good one I bought from Savers in Frankston when I drive there with my brother Rob to escape Coburg – it works!

The water for once comes on really hot so in hop I as old can be.

I love the water to relieve my aching old body that's got an old pot gut attached to the rest of itself. My baggy eyes I love because everyone in my old family's got hay fever 24/7. I'm just one of them, man!

I lie in the hot as hot as hot lasts which this night is just on thirty minutes maximum. I wash my hair with time passing mixed with Dettol which I mistook for Cedel. It isn't. I dry the self down in front of the two-bar heater and feel very privileged indeed. I put on my rags again and swear for ten minutes endeavouring to ignite the gas stove.

I put on hot boiling water and enjoy eggs upon crumpets as I study my bills on the warped kitchen tabletop. I wished I had a friend and not phone disconnection again.

From eight this morning time hummed and purred and the kids wrote imaginatively and bettered their prose after it was completed by reading their great work aloud out in the pong courtyard made of mountains of cigarette butts the Preps have enjoyed and spat out in their fiery determination to get lung cancer; the sharing was exciting and the kids read from their work luxuriantly, interestingly and unselfishly.

Our Principal had promised the school would have a word with Office Works and get the year's work put in a binder that the kids would show to their drunken or stoned or both parents but he always forgets what he says and always promises what I can't remember. The last English lesson of my day was unendurable; the kids who are so clever upon the left hand side of their brain can be irreversibly destructive upon the right hand side; and all Hell broke loose about ten to four when Darren complained that Tex had been given too much praise for his new poem that analysed family rape. Darren spat hard upon Tex and they then resorted to fisticuffs that a work experience girl called Tony filmed for Arts Mentone.

It was just awful to see a one-armed boy of thirteen

use a woodwork hammer on an old colleague. I was sick of the brawling and fuming and gouging on so I went and sat out on Sickening Road on the tarry footpath where it's awful but at least I didn't have to see them hurt each other. I watched the parents hang around and brawl just like their progeny. I missed the sensation of peace.

It was eleven in the morning and I went down to Barkly Square Plaza to shove some home-on-the-range into my meter; you get three hours on the house but then booked $64 if you stay over the limit. Boil Street has a bit of parking for staff right outside it on the asphalt footpath but it is all so higgle-de-piggledy I never park my depressing Honda Civic there. I'd never get it out.

I found my car – miracle in itself – and shoved a week's wages in the awful meter and immediately felt regret that so much shrapnel had disappeared down time's great slot. I wandered like the dead into the disgusting front eating bit and regretted being there, too.

I observed suicidal newly arrived detainees set up food poisoning outlets and eagerly vend dubious pork sausages or inedible noodles made of tetanus mixed with cat gut.

The folks eating had no manners and all fed just like hogs-at-trough. They snout things in rather than stoop to silver wear or even cutlery made of plastic to plough more revolting filth into themselves.

So noisy with loathe some chomping and gutsing and nobody reading. The stalls pump out mince or giddiness and lonely souls resort to eating because it's better than reading. I purchased a ninety-cent chocolate health biscuit whose wrapper informed me eighty per cent of its purchase price would go to The Horn Of Africa. I was relieved about that?

I sipped a hot cocoa and walked up the plaza gawking at confidence persons demonstrating little helicopters that are flown by a battery-driven wand; I wanted one for my son and shall buy him one today. The gentle objects hummed in a pleasant manner and lifted up or else zoomed sideways or even down in what I think is called a down-draught – anyway they were exciting to be sure. A few people were buying them and became happy for a fraction of a second, which is life's aim, surely to God who is a toy helicopter. I can't wait to get one for my young son.

Because I had a bit of free time I just sat on my bottom-end on a chair in the plaza and gazed at every one of us. Who are we all? Why do we buy gent's suits that neatly tear right in half whenever we sit down? Does it matter, quality of garments I mean?

The father of the tomahawk haircut boy was there, just standing there or sitting there, he had a funny slouching thing going on in him so it could've been either, actually, slouching/standing which used to be called in my day 'loitering with intent to commit a felony'. Wasn't he the arsehole who 41 years ago kicked the hard-pumped vinyl soccer ball into my head and broke my nose for me? And he wasn't contrite about it was he?

Nowadays his son wears the old man's mohawk quivers, glues the idiotic things onto his basalt skull in an effort to compliment his moronic father.

It is an uneasy moment when I recognise his father who now toils in the I.T. Industry and drives an up dated BMW navy blue coupe which he always parks right next to Brian's solar driven pushbike with a sun-driven tool kit. 'You still hangin' round here?' is all he intones, looking at me beneath his contempt. 'You have to teach somewhere,' is all I can come up with as he scratches his neck bunion with an impressive driving mitt.

The teachers work back every single day to show martyrdom. They are in there emailing prisoners to depress their spirits. They are trying to locate the missing air hockey disk, the one that's warped with a bite through it. I go home and attend a meeting about 7pm at the Chinese milk bar where the family want me to teach them English. This is my local shop where I buy my toilet paper and food to go with it. I don't like them much but I have nothing to lose so I go in.

I go out the back with an exercise book each for the guy who runs the joint and give him a pencil out of his own stock. We sit together in no heating whilst his exhausted family serve shop and sell canned everything. After two hours of him screaming and biting his own hand he has written 'dog' in English. He can't even pronounce 'dog' in Chinese. He stuffs round using the microwave oven to heat himself up several frozen pies then drowns the cold pastry and volcanic mince with Soy.

'Ah!' he adds, peering right into the mince, 'Not bad!' 'Now that is pretty good English, Ah So!' I say to him, but unfortunately he is all Soy. The filthy table is now full of babies that his mother deposits there in order to change them right under my protesting white nose. The amount of shit!

The fat Asian babies gargle and writhe as their shit is packed in toilet paper and then they are all thrown to bed. We go back to nouns and adverbs, that he enjoys. 'What rhymes with sphincter?' he asks very sweetly indeed but the fact is I can't think of a thing. The vast amount of baby shit-smell has sickened me and made English seem rather superfluous. He has been writing mostly in Chinese for the past hour and tells me midst a pile of revision that he was in tears once on an ocean liner when his great grandfather admitted to him he had witnessed the invasion of China by the Japanese.

He grumpily extracted a protesting twenty-dollar note out of his back pants that housed thousands of them and in a marked manner tossed it my way, in the exact way a leper would wipe its backside on *The Herald*.

An Eternal Meeting

Although it is only ten in the morning it feels more like the end of Time. And there is no sense of time passing at the grimmest gathering of the grimmest educators ever put collectively into one spot. The clock keeps showing ten and no other discernible hour; there never was another hour and it is highly unlikely there will be one until the closing down of All. They are already emailing each other in the utmost seriousness at the mortal stroke of ten on a Monday morning. Not that it is real morning. More like real morphine because that is the effect of educators posing ever more questions.

All sip percolated black coffees with a most studious expression that also has no answers in regard to teenage behaviour such as the incineration of the dove in a waste paper bin the other day during physical education. It wouldn't have been very relaxing for the dove who struggled desperately against its ignition and unasked for combustion; it cooked blackly out in the middle of the asphalt community volleyball court. Volleyball is the only subject which is compulsory.

The greatest grimness coats and chokes me and we all watch the clock overhead bully us into a minute past ten although that minute hand shall take no prisoners. The staff I've seen for decades but I can never learn any of their befuddling names and confuse them constantly with the titles of products like Bon Ami or Cadbury's Dairy Milk Chocolate. The teachers look like cleaning agents and I can envisage each of them scouring a stain off their carpets at home.

The clothing of the teachers differs from my eternal poverty-look. The ladies wear apple-coloured jackets with trendy fawn pants with a bell-bottom to them with their hair up. The chaps wear Fidel Castro revolutionary denims with a blinding white T-shirt over that with expensive sunglasses on top which they talk through using fashionable educational clichés such as 'one on one' meaning two human things talking.

Two of the teachers have screeching terriers that are soundly tethered to the leg of the table and these annoying things yap all through the meeting just to render it even more trying. It is my feeling here that we aren't paid to teach so much as endure two-hour meaningless meetings out of which nothing comes but a vast need for strong drink.

Brian Epstein our indefatigable principal looks flushed. He stands up in utter silence only to sit down again then mop his perspiring face with a red flag-like handkerchief. He is having a bad day and he looks all in before it has started. He has been at the helm for forty years and appears to know every single child who's entered our hallowed walls for he is forever singing out their names either in the courtyard or inside the eternally chained toilet where the loo paper is old hard-folded curriculum paper on a nail.

He is bowed over his indecipherable notes written from a memory that doesn't go anymore; the tiredness of his body is palpable and the weariness of his droopy eyelids is such that when they come down it is actually not so easy to raise them up again in order to read a thing. I don't understand how he can do the requirements of his long day, nor does he, poor object of hope in the face of four decades of mockery.

'I've actually already been to a funeral today which is the death by overdose of one our mother-parents who I thought had kicked smack; but as you know that isn't so easy as is supposed by non-users such as newsreaders or those who run milk bars.'

'You're drifting Brian. Stay on course!' calls out a morose teacher.

'It was quite hard meaning terrifying since she was so young and during second term had become an eager volunteer for Geography. We don't know really where she lived. The service was anonymous. Any questions?'

No one put up their questioning palm.

'She was detected deceased in a cheap motel by its Hindustani cleaner who now cleans for us I think you'll find. His name of course is Toby. Uncle Toby. There have been so many accidental heroin overdoses in Sickening Road it is remarkable the trams run on time.'

'Where are we going with this, Brian?' questioned someone.

'No, she was very special and really put in the hard stuff right in the old limb. I cried because I had no limb until I met a principal who had no school. She drank white wine a lot as well as her heroin habit so I screwed a new bottle into her unmarked grave and scratched her first name on it. Now on to the latest Victorian Education Department demands to fix our toilets. Has anyone read the latest emails from the senator behind this unnecessary pressure?'

A few arms sailed like beanpoles attached to their morning lattes

Miss Limbs spoke up with a voice on her like the cost of living; she teaches Ethics In Practice and the gossip at the hall is hot that she is making a run as principal and there are some who say she has the numbers. 'I rather believe The Victorian Education Department wants us to stay in Sickening Road as we are but to put in place a new structure of ...'

'Toilets?' droned Cassidy who teaches table tennis.

'Well no not toilets because as we all know The Mistress Of Urine is away on permanent leave in Thailand so that means we all of us have to hang on till we get home, which is a bit of a nuisance, but what they want is to transform our revolutionary college into a traditional high school and I'm very much afraid that would include a timetable.'

The staff gasped.

Brian had to interrupt which hardly came as a surprise. 'But our charter is to fill the gaps where kids come in to us who have assaulted police, usually women in Brunswick who toil as prostitutes. What earthly use would it be to the Victorian Education Department if we just become a standard school that makes sense?'

Hear! Hear!

'What we have at my helm is a rabbit hutch and in that hutch is a god damned hare! With our specially honed skills because most of us come from Melbourne University is to not lead children into a forced set of values but just respect and listen to them until they get their VCE.'

Hear! Hear!

The very crucially most important Monday Morning Meeting then became a noisome rackety cloud of theories on nuclear disarmament and breakthrough Welsh philosophers like Bertrand Russell. It was a crazed discussion that shot off on a billion tangents and I got away to the pantry, which I've discovered after 41 years, and made myself a very strong black coffee to take away even though I work there. My mind was very tired even at only ten in the morning. After the meeting was over I had a word with Brian Epstein about the boywho had screamed at me yesterday as well as given me the finger with only one arm.

He had improvised its wizened point and made it stick right up at me right in my teeth. Brian laughed in uproar at my being put out by Darren yesterday; and said, 'You should count yourself very fortunate Dickins to be told to go and fuck yourself by a young boy with one arm, because you have now been told to go and get fucked in every possible language including pantomime.'

I tried to tell him the review was proceeding apace despite the constant abuse of me but as I tried to catch his eye; he put it in a jar. He only has one. He then put on his black leather eye patch and went across drizzling Sickening Road for a Vietnamese salad roll you need a pick to break.

It is now again and the whole of Sickening Road is eating a salad roll one yard in width from Viet Cong Bakeries on the busy corner of Moreland Road. You can hear them chomping hours later because it takes hours to jaw your way through imitation Western food here with the purple salad onion completely impenetrable as well as the yard of shredded fresh carrot not even a pony could hope to penetrate.

I am getting stuck into one of them again right next to the hall with teachers at their break trying to get out of the limited space car park in front of the building without luck. They tend to get stuck there and are then forced to gnaw their buns in the front seat. I am determined not to get my muck everywhere today and use a plastic fork to impale sprigs of spring onion that slide over each back tooth of mine like a quoit landing on a stand.

I ordered cheese and tomato and frozen lettuce and am chomping into the foot-thick of the object in my willingness to live another week and get some nutrition into me in order to do stuff like get up a hill or put up with another insufferable tram ride home – that is where I need strength!

I go back to my next lesson which has just this second been cancelled because of a bus ride to Phillip Island; no one told me a thing and I just had Darren writing at his most experimental before the break and the boy bard Darren who with Darren shows real poetic dash. Darren was sitting there looking at me but considering poetry and we had made up with our eyes. That meant a lot to me that there were no hard feelings after he cursed me and of course threatened me with murder. It was only a bit of fun really, nothing but hot air so who cares? Not yours truly!

One teacher kicked rather than knocked on my door and grabbed furiously Darren's personal computer and slammed the lid down it went with all of Darren's limited sticky fingerprints all over it, the only remaining evidence of our writing workshops that he'd been enjoying – me too!

'Come on you!' she whined as she wrenched the personal computers out of his grasp to his and my shock. 'We're going to Phillip Island!' I went out the room with them and waved hooroo to the school bus as they tore off together leaving me with not a soul. I wondered what I'd get up to with no one to teach but my mind proved dull as dogma. There are no mind games at Boil; they can't afford them. Preps are taught boxing and computer skills from Day One. They do a fruit drive on Fridays so the kids of parents who forget to do their lunches and cordial bottle actually have nutrition and grow into more happy teachers like me. I learned the lesson in humility by trying on a thousand kinds of schools then discovering the right one in my neighbourhood.

They say I can work here till I'm 65 so that means only three years to go until I retire and get buried. That's okay with yours truly and nowadays I just take one screaming match at a time and enjoy my barbecue chop of a night in front of Channel Ten. Every single child who turns up at our gate is holy because they know learning is for them and that we are for them forever and ever amen.

The new way of my teaching technique was to follow Buddhism that escorted my ego to the wastepaper basket and instantly topped me up with a social unselfishness that is nigh on perfect. It happens to be a really new thing I discovered via my nightly dreams of global equality.

Even 42 years ago I had these recurring visions of self-effacement instead of Facebook; where the global community know in the instant whether you said a thing, remembered a thing, saw how you cowered or were courageous in the public eye of the all-seeing camera of loneliness.

I used to wake at my rental room in George Street and sit with my fellow tenant and write the beginnings of new literature upon the hideous kitchen table, using a biro and a notebook to capture thoughts for the starts of sentences fresh as new-baked buns in the local cake shop.

The inventions made me high and also 42 years ago I

read every single poem composed by Pablo Neruda who invented practically a revolutionary way to think, not so much in English because I believe he was Spanish, actually, but the translations I studied influenced every aspect of my mind. I took from this immortal bard the sense that everything is miraculous and that every atom is fresh and individualistic as a grin. I was so in love with Mr Neruda that I one day collided with a George Street lamp pole whilst reading him in his latest book.

I tried to love everything like an undrugged hippie and not to hold any prejudices. I went to the movies with motivational teachers and that helped. Through the divinity of their all-seeing eyes I connected with imagery in a way uncluttered by voices or analysis that leans so heavily on the English Voicebox.

In those formative days I endeavoured to live in the moment and even my reading was revolutionary, almost abstract because I borrowed various volumes from Coburg Library that in many senses contradicted themselves but I wanted as a young guy to probably read everything ever published and bear it all in mind for future reference.

I read widely and lived narrowly because I didn't wish to lose my virginity until I met my girlfriend. I did one day as she was selling tickets for the Red Cross on a stool in Bourke Street and we got to chatting and she invited me on the spot to drop over at her Mum and Dad's house in Box Hill the next Sunday for cake and tea but when I called by I could see her father frantically on her in the front bedroom. Clearly they were never Christians.

We went out once or twice after that sighting but she did give me something to read which I have to this day in my library in Coburg. It is *The Practical Guidebook To Wardrobe Restoration* by Dale Carnegie, and it went to many editions. I committed it to memory and can quote extensively from it today if requested.

42 years is a lot of teaching under the bridge but nothing is any different in Melbourne except it's not there anymore.

The other evening I endeavoured to re locate the GPO in Elizabeth Street as I had a bunch of mail to post, bills mostly and I still have 'Bill Night'.

The Review

The evening for the review came at long last and kids I really didn't think would want to make fools of themselves on stage actually weren't too bad for children who hadn't put on make-up before or confronted their first audience. The moment the crowd comes in on you can be appalling for both parties in my experience.

The kids managed to study their own miraculous lines and remember their own scatological songs. I could easily hear them running through the program in the dingy back room of the tiny theatre in Carlton. Loads of eager parents hanging around armed with mobile cameras to record. Two men boiling up hot dogs and another two men buttering crispy rolls. People putting last touches on sincere backdrops and decorating the curtains and making sure they flounced.

Most of the Boil Street teachers I assumed detested me still did. But I didn't care about any of that; perhaps it was all in my mind, the paranoia and meaningless sensitivity of thinking you don't fit in. We all do.

It was a quarter-to-eight and every single ticket sold so there were one hundred and twenty chairs altogether with parents all dressed up in their best clutching their just-printed programs, straining their eyes to take a peek at their own children's names set in tiny type. Parents smiling but not smugly in anticipation of something fantastic about to happen in a second or less than that. Theatre is made of excitement. Boy, was there excitement!

So much hubbub and putting on of green wigs in the cramped dressing room and kids mumbling their lines and working out cues. The director I hated once just looked tired and honest and normal. I'm sure I was envious of her teaching prowess and that was why we had a blow-up. All my fault just as everything is all my fault. She resembled Mother Mary giving the kids mercy. She looked such a noble leader!

I sat in my purchased chair and put my glasses on to read my program that included cartoons I'd drawn that looked crude although when doing them I thought they were the work of a genius. I'm no genius just a man which is all I ever wanted to be; whatever they are they are here to help battle illiteracy. I want to help.

I couldn't remember any of the teachers' names and I suppose that is how you get being a teacher of ten thousand types of schools and twenty thousand kinds of kids. From brutal to hyper to funny to cruel to talented to hell and kindergarten. I wished I had been a decent kindergarten teacher, that's all. I'm better with babies because I've never grown up. I can't. I'm an artist. But suddenly I remembered all their names!

It was now packed to overflowing with excited mums and delirious dads who just couldn't sit still as the house-lights went down by torturous degrees. An enormous giddy-green goblin came on made of papier-mâché. The crowd clapped loudly, swiftly, uproariously just seeing it shuffle forward to the dusty front pews.

The teachers all stood and whistled and stomped.

I whistled and stomped with them as the naïve big goblin huffed its chest and prop smoke billowed from its cartoon yet real nostrils. Music seemed Chinese with heaps of mandolins and little firecrackers all over the place: incense lent by the local church with no real rush to give it back. This was community theatre with hope in it and not propaganda. It was unpretentious fun and full of life. I was so uplifted.

A Chinese dragon slithered on that touched the ceiling almost of the theatre and it joined in with the dragon as a sort of motif before the actual character sketches started. The monologue to start the scenes was written by the boy with one arm and he learnt it and performed it without a solitary nerve. He got a big clap and he took a neat bow and there were a few tears, don't worry, just seeing him show daring. He was heroic!

Other kids played bored street characters with instantly recognisable accent and attitude that got appropriate responses, not just chuckling but open-mouthed-staring as though to say 'how do you know I said that?' Or else 'God I know where you got that from!'

Lonely sketches unashamedly brief as loneliness always is. Characters drawn from 7 Elevens and bedside vigils. Things you overhear at gravesides or bus stops, same thing. Bleak and tender lines filched from death who doesn't want that sentence back.

Sophisticated dialogue taken at knife-point from bitter family break-ups then sewn into their script in order to give the parents a jolt. It was jolt-writing. I had nothing to do with it.

Musical interludes of cornet and piano with the maths teacher playing improvisational trombone in a pool of impromptu light near the battered old community piano with a prop pot of beer on top of it made in the craft class at school and that received a big laugh soon as it was lit. Everything was comical.

I couldn't remember where the edited writing came from or how it was cut or how the kids managed to look so beautiful in their home-made policeman's costumes or bank robber outfits or how that brat girl I hated in Year 7 looked like the relaxed artiste on stage after so many disrupted classes where she bit her tutors and slagged on me one day near the photocopier – I'm sure I deserved it and now wondered why I didn't pay her any respect when I'd heard she had it hard at home.

There were a few dropped lines, a few stumbles, the prop kettle didn't work and the elephant made of orange garbage bags wasn't so scary but the show got claps all through and the scenes of home-gown pathos received the sorts of tears of love that just leap out of eyes that stare at children displaying all that potential. Some of the performers really looked the part and not just kids mucking around to pass their exams. Some were so brilliant I thought they could possibly become professional artists when they left Boil Street Special School. Wouldn't that be something?

It was over and all the kids are screaming over a Coke that the school has shouted them and the principal is crying with pride and the director and I are shaking palms and the kids are resting on the bleachers and glitter is in their cheeks and the strobe is still on and mums are handing out baked spuds and handing me one and someone is thanking me for helping out with grammar and punctuation.

'We did it. We pulled it off, by George!' laughs our principal and his wife gives him a hug and a cup of hot tea but he has a cold ale with the staff. A bathtub is jerked into the centre of the space and people are told to help themselves but there aren't many takers, not even the Year 12s, and that seems funny because they're always raving on about the latest boutique beers from Japan and Broadmeadows. One of the kids gives me a powerful hug and whispers 'I wish you was my Dad!' He is a Year Eight kid who hasn't got a father. In the moment I very nearly replied 'I wished you were my son,' however I didn't, thank God, because I have a splendid son of my own and I don't imagine he'd like a rival. I catch the Moreland rocket home and everyone on it's a ticket-inspector. Sixty-six of them. I loved them too!

I munched the usual baked beans and hopped in the bath and was very surprised to see so much blue ink on my body in the hot water; but it was from all the kids in the review I wrote with them, who had printed their wobbly autographs on me after the show and I hadn't even noticed them. As I hadn't even noticed anything much in a long life of pleasing myself much more than learning from kids at a thousand sorts of schools.

After that I got up as I always do after a minute's worth of repose and preposterous nightmares and put the kettle on. I sipped tea and re-read my latest threats of disconnection with Optus and felt better. What had I learnt but the lesson we all ignore until it's too late almost. Humility and its place in my resurrection. Amen.

The House of Welcome

Four long decades back I and another young teacher named Robert were sent as Special English Teachers to the House Of Welcome in grotty Brunswick Street and just the bite of disinfectant took the wind out of my sails as we both stepped in there. Cleaners were dousing the vast concrete slabs of the dining area with liberal buckets of near full strength White King to eradicate sin.

The eradicated sins comprised being perpetually begrimed and never washing your clothing and never brooming ashes from your teeth and never saying thanks and never saying 'Hi'. As I said earlier in my teachers' memoirs the world in my opinion is divided into just two halves. Those who are pleased to say 'Hi!' and those who never do. I'm a 'Hi!' guy myself' and adore to see kids smile, particularly when their spelling picks up.

We only had to be there one week but it was the hardest week of my young existence. The lonely men crawled in like sub-human molluscs and the ladies looked like slugs in busted shoes. So filthy and unloved, almost dare I say it: unlovable. The ladies chainsmoked in the courtyard and swore a great deal of the time, maybe because their husbands were philanderers, it's hard to say.

In the writing room the poor were delivered of a

crummy black lead pencil and a notebook on a string with the same crummy pencil all snagged in it.

They all sat, already exhausted at nine in the morning in the common room sort of thing and stared unseeingly at note pads and ugly squat pencils hooked up to them. The priest blessed them then we wrote our feelings down before morning tea. Which tasted like lukewarm Pine O Cleen.

Robert and myself didn't say very much, we just asked them to write today's date somewhere upon their pages, plus their identities and any possible telephone contacts and we started out writing nonsense poetry in the key of Edward Lear. It took an hour without a single chuckle to print by nervy hand a rhyme or two but in the end we shared and I have to say they loved it.

To see their shagged-out hard-done-by countenances grin from ear to lopped-off-ear with mirth and true satisfaction that they could write too and make the group laugh was a breakthrough. Although their wonky hand-lettering was pretty hard to understand it was miraculous that they did it. We read out the front, so far out the front in fact that we were practically right on the footpath!

To see their unmirthful eyes become amused and to share the inventions of the just-for-fun poems was the whole genesis of the teaching technique I have striven for all my life. It is the pleasure of the company of English the language. Through it you may say the thing that hurts, that just about is killing you, or in a different whim or with a slightly different pencil you can break all hearts if you feel like that, kind of thing. I'm speaking of Drama.

It was long ago that first day 42 years ago at The House Of Welcome and the harsh aspects were the way the officials vigorously mopped Dettol all across the cement floor we were sitting at so that the pong of it rose up like several serpents and bit you in the soul. Fifteen staff mopped and worried at the sinful cement under the poor's unslippered feet as we wrote together.

One bag lady penned her memoirs on a big hunk of tar paper over the course of a lifetime's worth of remembrance; she lived as a waif in The Wimmera and had captured a million quotations from the scrub and blended them with a fable that had come to her via the grace of God. She explained this to the unminding group, who by now were beavering away like mad, their stubby pencils and coagulated pens darting down not merely rhymes but writing in a thousand styles, all original, straight off the footpath where lots of rivetting tales get conceived only in the utterance.

When they ate mostly they ceased literature but a few kept on writing even with a bent fork full of hot carrot in it, almost using hot canned muck to remember life with. A woman wrote exclusively on the subject of her many evictions; when she shared they wept with equal vivid recollections. She sure read convincingly and didn't use a microphone, not that one was available for a live reading anyway. Everything was done on the floor.

The lunch was awful food but mostly they gulped a fair bit of it down. Robert fibbed that he's already eaten his grub but a Mother Superior figure made him complete it anyway. She stabbed her fat white chunky digit at the tucker and shouted at my fellow English teacher-rounds. 'Eat it!' And he did though he was pretty much full in the tummy.

At the end of that special week their writing was duly dully photocopied and stapled into a book and they organised a public reading but the food was the exact same canned muck which I happen personally to love. I love my muck!

I realised teaching is noblesse oblige and have taught actually in the very same way my loving patents have joked with me all my days; I talk directly to the kids, I know teachers are not these days supposed to do that, they are to be sort of friendly but demonstrate the fact they are professionals and not friends.

The Learning Lies in Eyes

Education is all in the eyes and nowhere much else. As in the beginning of small talk with the wee babe doing handstands on the mother's knees or down the beach where its is windy and tennis racquets where once my little brother Robert aged eight invented the rules for underwater tennis. Fun is what teaches you anything and despite genius levels on the internet and instant access into I.T. Sections of Rapid Cash the difference between thought and cliché is eyes. The eyes have it.

Once for a term I taught poetry at MLC where my supervisor insisted upon me writing my poem outlines on a personal computer and sending them an inch away to the snow-blind Year 7s. It just didn't work because the only way I can do it, teach that is, is to have eye contact.

But my mother and father demonstrated learning in all its myriad expressions merely with a half smile or a quarter shrug; every single gesture of theirs was a very powerful language, actually, and you got the idea as soon as they squinted at you. I have gone into the classroom similarly armed with affection for youth.

What's education exactly? Is it schools and universities and insufferable kindergartens?

My experience of them as pupil dead-bored and teacher for forty years is that you learn more in bed.

Bed's the best teacher I ever had. The visions or dreams copped in slumber are so memorable, even amusing and surreal. The schools I've suffered most in aren't funny; in fact funniness has no spot in them nor has my hero Edward Lear who wrote whimsically from dawn till dark because he felt like it.

Most schools I've been the guest poet at aren't poetic. Those venerable institutions respect clinical depression much more than a pupil who has enough gas in the tank to be a successful stand-up or an A-List tragedian.

Some places I've taught grammar at can't speak. Others can but only gibberish or secondhand gossip; not that any writer worth his salt turns up the nose at hearsay. It is the stuff of true drama because people in the main hate one another, particularly kindergarten teachers.

Learning is to do with seeing. People can't see the wood for the mobile.

As I've grown down and not up all I'm concerned with is joy. The rest can bag its head. I wake and thank God (who is Corn Flakes) that I'm animate. Everything else is downhill from there on. My long life has been a love poem dedicated to agony. I loved my wife and she left me. I love my son who writes better than me. I was hospitalised for anxiety yet I live deliberately in Melbourne, the home of it.

My idea of teaching is listening. I hear my son laughing from his room where he's always listening to jazz overnight on the wireless I bought him a couple of Christmases ago. He taught me happiness today just hanging around with 'The Old Cheese' as he calls me sometimes – with him being 'Young Cheese'.

Too often in schools whether rich or poor the whole thing suffers from worthiness rather than worthlessness which is truly something to strive for. Last night I viewed a boring hour-long program upon The ABC depicting wealthy parents shouting enraptured when they read their son's or daughter's exam results that showed in some cases 100%. In one bizarre encounter you the television consumer beheld a laid-back boy of twelve metres waddle back to high school to glow in the magnificence of his record marks. His fat and hysterical English coordinator mounted him on the spot for being the greatest achiever since Satan.

My father taught me patience and my mother how to write my name. What else do you need to make a million? Last year at a community school the Year 7s I tried hard to have a rapport with used texting to express themselves. I couldn't understand a syllable of it partly because it isn't English or Grammar nor is it meant to be. It is tough.

When I was a happy little chap I ran to State School actually because I confused my teachers with Mum and Dad and assumed we'd all grow old together making daisy chains and catching bronchial pneumonia. It wasn't really like that but I am a Romantic.

In some school I've had my life threatened and gone

home disappointed they didn't go on with it. In others I've had infinitesimal girls escort me personally upstairs to teach other slightly bigger girls of six years old how to write verse. Some schools have loved me and others have detested my style and even my face.

I have been bullied by teachers far more than by students. I have felt unwanted in poor schools because the principals drive BMWs. I have fainted out of boredom at the Monday Morning Meeting at high-minded but low-friendly community colleges where the teachers seem smugger than Power Ball winners.

My life or lives as a teacher is not remarkable but contains stories I felt like writing in order to appal (hopefully) or entertain my reader. I've only loved one person and that's my reader.

In my opinion there shouldn't be teachers because preps know more than they do and they are better to look at. All teachers are born ugly. That was a decision of God. And what is God? He sharpens the pencils for angels with no money for lunch.